CHRISTIAN THOUGHT

A Brief History

CHRISTIAN THOUGHT
A Brief History

Edited by
Adrian Hastings
Alistair Mason &
Hugh Pyper

OXFORD
UNIVERSITY PRESS

OXFORD
UNIVERSITY PRESS

Great Clarendon Street, Oxford OX2 6DP

Oxford University Press is a department of the University of Oxford.
It furthers the University's objective of excellence in research, scholarship,
and education by publishing worldwide in

Oxford New York

Auckland Bangkok Buenos Aires Cape Town Chennai
Dar es Salaam Delhi Hong Kong Istanbul Karachi Kolkata
Kuala Lumpur Madrid Melbourne Mexico City Mumbai Nairobi
São Paulo Shanghai Singapore Taipei Tokyo Toronto

with an associated company in Berlin

Published in the United States
by Oxford University Press Inc., New York

© Oxford University Press 2002

Database right Oxford University Press (maker)

First published 2002

British Library Cataloguing in Publication Data

Data available

Library of Congress Cataloging in Publication Data

Data available

ISBN 0-19-280280-1

1 3 5 7 9 10 8 6 4 2

Typeset in Pondicherry, India, by
Alliance Interactive Technology
Printed in Great Britain by
Clays Ltd
Bungay, Suffolk

Contents

CONTENTS

Introduction

'CHRISTIAN THEOLOGY MAY WELL BE IN A HEALTHIER, MORE INTERNALLY COHERENT, AND LESS SCHISMATIC STATE THAN HAS BEEN THE CASE FOR MANY CENTURIES.' With these words Adrian Hastings ends the masterly survey of Christian thought in the 20th century that concludes this volume. Sadly, his death in May 2001 means that his active contribution to Christian thought in the 21st century has been lost to us. It is gratifying, then, that it was editing the *Oxford Companion to Christian Thought*, from which the following chapters derive, which led him to this positive opinion. Somewhat to his surprise, as he admitted, it became clear that, despite the range of pressures that modern secularism and global capitalism bring to bear, this is not a survey of a dying tradition which will soon be of merely historical interest. On the contrary, an appreciation of the roots of the continued vitality and diversity of Christian thought, despite the foolishness and wickedness to which its history too often bears witness, is relevant to all those, Christian and non-Christian, who will be shaping the thought of the next century and beyond.

Christian thought is an elusive concept to define. Christians have always done more than think, of course, and they think about more than theological issues. As Christianity in its various forms became the dominant religion in Western Europe, politics, law, science, art, and engineering, for example, were developed by people professing a Christian commitment. By the same token, Christians have had to change their minds or at least update their arguments throughout the last two millennia as social and cultural changes have come and gone and as new information and historical events have arisen. The debates over major discoveries in astronomy and biology may be the most familiar examples, but the morality of moneylending and slavery, the understanding of marriage and attitudes to Judaism, for instance, have also been rethought in response to changing circumstances.

Yet Europe has never had a monopoly on Christian thought, and the chapters in this book on the Syriac, Armenian, and Eastern Orthodox traditions bear witness to bodies of thought which developed their insights in response to different political and intellectual pressures. Today these traditions are part of a new kind of global conversation between Christians that has revealed the restrictedness of the view from Europe and North America.

The expansion of Europe through colonialism and missionary activity into the Americas and the rest of the world led to encounters with unfamiliar societies which have in turn contributed to new and vibrant forms of Christian thought. Intellectual fashions and preoccupations change too, and Christian thinkers have tried to adapt Christianity to such new ideas, or to assimilate them into Christianity, or to produce a Christian counter to them. Often they have argued fiercely among themselves as to which strategy should be adopted. Political and other disagreements have also set Christians against each other. Whatever the outcome or the rights and wrongs, as argument rages the range of Christian thought is expanded and modified and this is reflected in condensed form here.

This volume consists of a series of chapters which form the backbone of the *Oxford Companion to Christian Thought*, anchoring and pulling together the discussion of the vast range of concepts and thinkers to be found there. They provide a way to understand the complex developments of thought over a historical period. As Christian thought cannot be neatly divided into chronological segments, certainly not simply by changes of century, overlap between the articles is inevitable. We hope that this allows the reader to follow the shape of various intellectual movements which may arise in one period, but bear their fruits in the next.

The survey begins with Pre-Constantinian thought in the 2nd and 3rd centuries. This is not to imply that there is no earlier Christian thought. The writers of the New Testament and other apostolic fathers are more than sufficient witnesses to that. However, it is as the New Testament takes shape and the church consolidates its identity that a new intellectual effort of interpretation and synthesis becomes necessary. It is the history of this effort that is explored in subsequent chapters in a way that takes seriously both the Eastern and Western traditions of Christianity as these diverge in later centuries.

Written by world-renowned experts on their periods, these chapters cumulatively give the context within which important Christian ideas arise and are modified in response to new conditions. In turn, these evolving ideas themselves fuel the intellectual and social movements which influence contemporary societies in a constant process of exchange. An overall sense of how ideas fit together and how the answers of one era provide the questions of the next can easily be lost in the mass of factual detail. Here each chapter acts, we hope, as a map to help with orientation in a potentially bewildering terrain.

On the other hand, one of the principal aims of such an overview is to introduce the reader briefly to concepts, movements, and people about which he or she will want to know more. *The Oxford Companion to Christian Thought*, *The Oxford Companion to the Bible*, and *The Oxford Dictionary of the Christian Church* are obvious places to go for such information, and they in turn will lead the reader to more specialist sources.

Many people have contributed time, energy, and expertise to enable this volume to appear, and Adrian Hastings's expressions of gratitude to the contributors, the editorial team and to Oxford University Press are warmly echoed here. All of these know how much it is thanks to his unique blend of incisive efficiency and imaginative scholarship that the contents of this book have reached their present standard of clarity and comprehensiveness, and acknowledge the gap which his death has left. It is fitting, then, that the last word should be his. We join him in repeating his characteristic wish from the Introduction to the *Companion* that readers of this book 'will find, among much that is enlightening, informative, and even amusing, some things that may well be true'.

HUGH S. PYPER
Leeds
27 January 2002

Editors & Contributors

Editors

The late Adrian Hastings was Emeritus Professor of Theology, University of Leeds, and previously Professor of Religious Studies, University of Zimbabwe. He was the Editor of the *Journal of Religion in Africa* for 15 years. He also edited a number of books including *Modern Catholicism* (1991) and *A World History of Christianity* (1999). His many other publications include a two-volume commentary on the documents of the Second Vatican Council (1968–9), *A History of English Christianity 1920–2000* (1986, 3rd edn 2001), *The Theology of a Protestant Catholic* (1990), *Robert Runcie* (1991), *SOS Bosnia* (1993), *The Church in Africa 1450–1950* (1994, a volume in the *Oxford History of the Christian Church*), and *The Construction of Nationhood* (1997).

Alistair Mason has recently retired as Senior Lecturer in Church History, University of Leeds. He is the author of *A History of the Society of the Sacred Mission* (1993), and editor of *Religion in Leeds* (1994).

Hugh Pyper is Head of School and Senior Lecturer in Biblical Studies, University of Leeds. He is the author of *David as Reader: 2 Samuel 12: 1–5 and the Poetics of Fatherhood* (1996) and editor of *The Christian Family: A Concept in Crisis* (1996).

Contributors

John Cavadini, Professor, Department of Theology, University of Notre Dame

Vigen Guroian, Professor of Theology and Ethics, Loyola College, Maryland, Baltimore

Susan Ashbrook Harvey, Associate Professor of Religious Studies, Brown University, Providence, Rhode Island

The late Adrian Hastings, editor

Seán F. Hughes, Department of Theology, University of St Thomas, Minneapolis-St Paul

John Kent, Emeritus Professor of Theology, University of Bristol

C. Hugh Lawrence, Emeritus Professor of Medieval History, University of London

Andrew Louth, Professor of Patristic and Byzantine Studies, University of Durham

John McGuckin, Professor of Early Church History, Union Theological Seminary, New York

Anthony Milton, Senior Lecturer, Department of History, University of Sheffield

Lloyd G. Patterson, Huntington Professor of Historical Theology Emeritus, Episcopal Divinity School, Cambridge, Massachusetts

Kallistos Ware, Lecturer in Eastern Orthodox Studies, University of Oxford, and titular Bishop of Diokleia

Claude Welch, Dean Emeritus and Professor of Historical Theology, Graduate Theological Union

Abbreviations

ARCIC	Anglican/Roman Catholic International Commission	Judg.	Judges
c.	circa	1, 2 Sam.	1, 2 Samuel
CD	Karl Barth, *Church Dogmatics*	1, 2 Kgs.	1, 2 Kings
col/s.	Column/s	1, 2 Chr.	1, 2 Chronicles
d.	died (with date)	Pss.	Psalms
DE	Degree on Ecumenism (Vatican II)	Prov.	Proverbs
DV	Dei Verbum (Vatican II)	Eccles.	Ecclesiastes
EH	Eusebius, *Ecclesiastical History*	Isa.	Isaiah
ET	English translation	Jer.	Jeremiah
GS	Gaudium et Spes (Vatican II)	Ezek.	Ezekiel
LG	Lumen Gentium (Vatican II)	Dan.	Daniel
LXX	Septuagint	Hos.	Hosea
NT	New Testament	Mic.	Micah
OT	Old Testament	Zech.	Zechariah
ST	Thomas Aquinas, *Summa Theologiae*	Mal.	Malachi
sv.	*sub verbo* (under the word)	1, 2 Esd.	1, 2 Esdras
vs.	versus	Tob.	Tobit

ARCIC   Anglican/Roman Catholic International Commission
c.   circa
CD   Karl Barth, *Church Dogmatics*
col/s.   Column/s
d.   died (with date)
DE   Degree on Ecumenism (Vatican II)
DV   Dei Verbum (Vatican II)
EH   Eusebius, *Ecclesiastical History*
ET   English translation
GS   Gaudium et Spes (Vatican II)
LG   Lumen Gentium (Vatican II)
LXX   Septuagint
NT   New Testament
OT   Old Testament
ST   Thomas Aquinas, *Summa Theologiae*
sv.   *sub verbo* (under the word)
vs.   versus

Biblical references

Gen.   Genesis
Exod.   Exodus
Lev.   Leviticus
Num.   Numbers
Deut.   Deuteronomy
Josh.   Joshua

Judg.   Judges
1, 2 Sam.   1, 2 Samuel
1, 2 Kgs.   1, 2 Kings
1, 2 Chr.   1, 2 Chronicles
Pss.   Psalms
Prov.   Proverbs
Eccles.   Ecclesiastes
Isa.   Isaiah
Jer.   Jeremiah
Ezek.   Ezekiel
Dan.   Daniel
Hos.   Hosea
Mic.   Micah
Zech.   Zechariah
Mal.   Malachi
1, 2 Esd.   1, 2 Esdras
Tob.   Tobit
Wisd.   Wisdom of Solomon
Ecclus.   Ecclesiasticus
1, 2 Macc.   1, 2 Maccabees
Sir.   Ecclesiaticus
Matt.   Matthew
Rom.   Romans
1, 2 Cor.   1, 2 Corinthians
Gal.   Galatians
Eph.   Ephesians
Phil.   Philippians
Col.   Colossians
1, 2 Thess.   1, 2 Thessalonians
1, 2 Tim.   1, 2 Timothy
Philem.   Philemon
Heb.   Hebrews
Jas.   James
1, 2 Pet.   1, 2 Peter
Rev.   Revelation

I

CANON AND CONSENSUS
Pre-Constantinian thought

≱ + ≱

L. G. Patterson

CHRISTIAN THOUGHT IN THE 2ND AND 3RD CENTURIES, before the change of government policy toward Christianity under Constantine, provokes differing reactions. The emergence of some consensus in Christian thinking, in the work of such figures as Justin Martyr, Irenaeus, Tertullian, Clement of Alexandria, and Origen, is sometimes hailed as addressing fundamental implications of the gospel, sometimes decried as introducing alien philosophical ideas or imposing ecclesiastical authority in matters of belief.

The developments to which these figures contributed are clear. Despite their differences, they worked towards establishing what would finally become the body of Christian scriptures—the Jewish writings and an eventually recognized collection of Christian writings—as the basis of Christian teaching. They also agreed in regarding the 'rule (*canon*) of faith' embodied in the confessions of faith used in preparation for baptism—the forerunners of later creeds—as the key to understanding these scriptures. Their exploration of scriptural teaching broadly established the agenda of their successors in the following centuries: the relation of God to the world and of the persons of the Godhead to each other, and the nature of evil, all in the context of the unfolding plan of salvation now approaching its completion with the coming of Christ and the gift of the Holy Spirit.

Neither these writers nor their successors were systematic theologians in any later sense. They are treated here in the light of the issues they addressed, with only the briefest reference to contradictory estimates of their work. For instance, we assume that the various confessional forms embodying the 'rule of faith' have their origin in such primitive proclamations and explanations of the new life in Christ, given through the Spirit in baptism, as Romans 6–8 and Matthew 28: 19, rather than that they were contrived to establish ecclesiastical authority over people's beliefs.

Again, when we see them in use, these confessions of faith include themes which differentiate them from the teachings of the various so-called Gnostic groups: they affirm God as creator of earth as well as heaven, Christ come in the flesh, salvation through the church, forgiveness, and Resurrection rather than 'knowledge'. But our writers are not to be seen as merely rejecting the teaching of their opponents as 'heretical' for questioning common belief. Indeed, much of the interest of the 'orthodox' writing of the period lies in its efforts to understand the secret teaching of the Gnostics and to meet its challenge through interpretation of the scriptures.

Finally, these writers, with their diverse knowledge and differing estimates of the issues discussed in the philosophical schools, were concerned with philosophy for its usefulness in exploring basic elements of Christian belief, not as constituting a framework within which to interpret the gospel.

✿ The early period

The collection of late 1st- and early 2nd-century writings, which the 17th-century French scholar Cotelier was perhaps the first to call 'apostolic fathers', includes works of considerable and diverse interest: letters of Clement of Rome, Ignatius of Antioch, and Polycarp of Smyrna, the visions of the *Shepherd of Hermas*, and an early liturgical manual called *Didache* (Teaching of the Twelve Apostles). These writings were not eventually included in the body of Christian scriptures, but they are invaluable additions to our knowledge of the life and thought reflected in those contemporary books that were later so included.

The designation of various 2nd-century writers as 'apologists' is justified by its use in the writings of Quadratus, Aristides, and Justin Martyr, and by implication in Theophilus of Antioch, Athenagoras, and Tatian, and certainly reflects the circumstances of a time when growing pagan opposition and government intervention called for reasoned accounts of Christianity. But the 'apologists' addressed not merely pagans but themselves and their Christian readers. It is with them that the processes of Christian thinking that will engage our attention begin to reveal themselves.

Justin Martyr stands out here in view of the extent and influence of his work. Convert from philosophy, catechist of the Greek-speaking Christian community at Rome, he was martyred *c.*165. His *Apology*, a broadside formally addressed to the co-emperors of the time, while necessarily simplified in presentation, gives a fair summary of his understanding of Christianity. The philosophical tradition has speculated that there is one God, whose Word is the source of cosmic order and the rational principle in humanity: the God of Israel is in truth the one whom the philosophers sought, and the Word has now become flesh in Jesus Christ and is responsible for the spread of the church (*Apol.* 9–10, 12–13). For Justin the Jewish writings are the 'scriptures' of the church (the Christian writings are not yet so regarded); and his proof of the truth of Christianity involves showing that what was prophesied in the scriptures is now being fulfilled in the events unfolding through the coming of Christ and, in anticipation, the culmination of the divine plan at the final judgement (ibid. 31–53). Meanwhile, through baptism and Eucharist we participate in the life of the risen Christ through the Spirit (ibid. 61–6). While Justin does not here refer to a confession of faith, basic elements of his catechetical teaching can clearly be seen behind his explanation of baptism into the triune name; and the account of his trial records the recitation of such a confession as an explanation of Christian belief (*Martyrdom of Justin and Companions*, in Stevenson 1985: 28–30).

Others of Justin's authentic surviving works spell out aspects of his teaching. A *Second Apology*, commonly regarded as an appendix to the first, states clearly that God is the only 'uncreated' reality (2 *Apol.* 6); while the later *Dialogue with Trypho the Jew*, chiefly devoted to showing that the Jewish Scriptures foretell the coming of Christ as understood by Christians, includes an account of his abandonment of the search for salvation through philosophy because he became convinced that the soul is 'created' and thus mortal (*Dial.* 5). It is in treating the issue of 'creation', with its philosophical implications of change, temporality, and even physicality, that Justin raises questions that will later be the subject of long debate among Christians. At a time when there is as yet no clear distinction in use between spiritual 'begetting' and 'creation' or 'generation,' Justin calls the Word 'created', unaware of the full dimension of the problem. Nor does he address such issues as the continuance of embodied existence after the Resurrection which the tradition has to deal with later. Nevertheless, with Justin we cross a threshold into a time when the concern of Christians to explain their faith to themselves as well as to others begins to raise rational issues not directly confronted before.

Irenaeus was bishop of the Greek Christian community at Lyons (Lugdunum) in Gaul. A native of Asia Minor, he was known in the Greek Christian community at Rome, and was a presbyter of Lyons when he succeeded bishop Pothinus on his death in the persecution of 177. He is assumed to have died *c.*195. Of Irenaeus' two surviving works, one is a brief catechetical *Explanation of the Apostolic Faith* (*Demonstratio*), which he described as a summary of the teaching of the other, the massive five books of 'Detection and Refutation of the Knowledge Falsely So-Called', commonly known by the title of its Latin translation: *Against Heresies* (*Adversus haereses*). Irenaeus is especially concerned with the secret teaching of the Christian Gnostic groups of Valentinians (of the western school of Ptolemy), and with the Marcionites. He also gives accounts of a wide variety of teachers, criticizing them for their use of philosophical ideas, while attributing their origin to the teaching of Simon Magus (Acts 8: 9–24), probably in dependence on lost works of Justin.

Irenaeus' treatment of the Valentinians shows them interpreting the same scriptures as used by Christians in general. In the Ptolemaic version of their teaching, they find scriptural evidence for the existence of a vast series of spiritual aeons constituting a divine *pleroma* or 'fullness' beyond the present world. The world was caused by the fall of the last of the aeons, Sophia (Wisdom), whose envious passion for the highest divine being brings forth a formless offspring, subsequently organized by a lesser creator into three orders: a physical order doomed to destruction, an imperfect psychic order to which the generality of Christians belong, and a spiritual order, the remnant seed of Sophia. Eventually, a saviour from the *pleroma* appears in the form of Jesus, to recall to their true place those who are spirituals by nature.

Irenaeus recognizes the appeal of this scheme when he frequently refers to it as his opponents' *hypothesis*, a plausible but untrue narrative. From Book 1 onwards he opposes to it the 'rule of faith (or truth)' everywhere accepted by the churches (*Adv. haer.* 1. 10. 1–2) as the key to the interpretation of the scriptures, now regarded as including the Christian writings. Though he can speak of the rule as 'our hypothesis', he identifies it as the apostolic *traditio* (*paradosis*) which is 'passed on' in the churches. He constantly insists that the 'rule' identifies the creator not as a lesser but as the only God, and the saviour as the Son of the creator and not an independent aeon. He has also in mind a larger series of issues with which, he suggests ironically, a person of greater insight—a 'Gnostic'—ought to be wrestling instead of denying the essentials of belief (1. 10. 3). Among these is the question of why the same God gave more than one covenant, and he will later go on to deal with the Marcionite view that the covenant of the law is the work of an evil God who condemns the disobedient, in contrast to that of the 'God and Father of our Lord Jesus Christ' who accepts sinners who believe.

Irenaeus' work was written in stages, giving rise both to repetition and to the introduction of new subjects. We may notice that Book 2 shows a surprising degree of dependence on rational argument proving that the divine must be one, and that, whether his opponents regard the ground of their *pleroma* or the *pleroma* itself as divine, they are 'rising beyond' human ability to penetrate the divine and erroneously picturing there the diversity of the created order (2. 1. 5, 8. 1–3, 13. 3–8). Book 3, the first of several later instalments, supports the claim of the 'rule' to be apostolic by pointing to the preservation in the churches, by the succession of bishops, of the apostolic traditions in contrast to the diversity and lateness of the teachings of his opponents (3. 3–5).

In Book 4 Irenaeus offers his basic reply to his opponents' view of the divine plan or *economy* (*oikonomia*) of salvation. Humanity, as created, was necessarily imperfect and needed growth and education before it could achieve existence 'according to the image and likeness' of the uncreated God (4. 38. 1–4). Moreover, humanity, as essentially possessed of 'self-determination' (free will), disobeyed and incurred mortality. The plan of salvation must, then, lead humanity freely to its destined perfection as well as reversing the consequences of disobedience. Thus the various stages of God's involvement with humanity lead to the coming of the Son or Word in the flesh in Christ as a *recapitulatio* (a 'new summing up') of humanity (Eph. 1: 10), so that the decrees of the law are cancelled and a renewed humanity is now capable of movement towards perfection 'according to the image and likeness' (e.g. 1. 10. 1; 3. 16. 6; 5. 21). In a phrase which runs through the work in various forms, in Christ 'the divine became human so that humanity might become divine' (e.g. 3. 10. 2, 19. 1; 4. 20. 5; 5 *praef.*).

In the final Book 5, a summary of many themes, Irenaeus looks forward to the outcome of the divine plan, and makes reference to the 'millenarian' tradition of his native Asia Minor, whereby a first resurrection of the saints will be followed by a thousand-year reign on a renewed earth before a final judgement. But his interpretation of the millennium reflects his vision of the perfection of humanity (5. 27–8), so that it serves as preparation for life 'according to the image and likeness of God', the words with which the work concludes.

Irenaeus says that his predecessors had not discovered enough about the teaching of their opponents to answer them (4. *praef.* 2), and he himself not only tries to be clear about that teaching but, despite inevitable rhetoric and invective, to deal with the issues it raises regarding essential elements of belief. He is perhaps most incisive in his treatment of the one divine nature and in his view of the relation of human freedom and divine initiative in the process of redemption. But he does not address Justin's outstanding problem of the 'created' Word: while he places Son and Spirit on the divine side of the gulf between divine and created, he avoids discussing their genesis. Similarly, while he clearly sets his anthropology of human freedom against Valentinian determinism, the restoration of the bodily unity of soul and flesh at the resurrection, while insisted upon, remains an unexplored question.

✿ The 3rd century

The writers dealt with so far have belonged to the Greek Christian communities that spread across the eastern Mediterranean and into Italy and Gaul. With Q. Septimius Florens Tertullianus of Carthage (*c.*160–*c.*225), and his early *Apology* of 196, we have evidence of the existence of Latin Christian communities in north-west Africa, already established with Latin translations of the Septuagint and the standard collection of Christian writings. But Tertullian and his Latin Christians did not think theirs a separate tradition of Christian thought. Bilingual himself, familiar with Justin and seemingly already possessing the Latin translation of Irenaeus, *Adversus haereses*, he is consciously dependent on his Greek predecessors. At the same time, attention to some major points will reveal the particular Latin perspective that Tertullian brings to the tradition.

His *Apology* uses themes of Justin's work, but greatly expands on the argument that the scriptures forecast events. These include not only the coming of Christ and the spread of the church but also (a display of the persistent Latin concern for Rome's historical destiny) contemporary troubles reflecting the coming judgement of God who, rather than the Roman deities, truly controls events (*Apol.* 20, 25–6). Again, using Irenaeus in a summary rejection of Gnosticism in *Concerning the Prescription of Heretics* (*De praescriptione haereticorum*) he employs a legal argument to rule any consideration of Gnostic views of the scriptures out of court since Gnostics do not believe the rule of faith (*Praes.* 15–19). Here too we find the starkest repudiation of reliance on philosophical ideas rather than belief (ibid. 7), though in other places he himself argues at length with the Valentinians and Marcionites, notoriously employs philosophical arguments, and regards religious beliefs as common to all human beings. None the less, the repudiation is an important reflection of ingrained Latin assumptions (as in Cicero and Virgil) that adherence to causes involves and requires unswerving personal commitment. These assumptions are reflected in Tertullian's view of the church as a community of the totally committed. This made him sympathetic to Montanist claims that a special gift of the Spirit is required for full commitment to Christ. It is also the start of the never-ending struggle among Latin Christians to explain the imperfect character of the body of believers.

Among aspects of Tertullian's thought, note should be taken of his treatment of the status of the Word, a question inherited from his predecessors. In his *Against Praxeas* (*Adversus Praxeam*) in particular, he faces a form of Monarchianism (or rejection of any division within the one divine nature) not dealt with by his Greek sources. Here he confronts more directly than does Irenaeus the problem of what it means that, the Father being the sole ungenerate, the clearly separate Word is generate and the agent of the divine presence in the created order. But here he relies on a Stoic notion of a quasi-physical divine substance in order to argue, one may think unsuccessfully, that the created Word is nevertheless somehow a part of the divine (*Prax.* 8).

If Tertullian marks the reception of major issues of contemporary Christian thought in the Latin Christian world of his time, Clement of Alexandria, roughly his contemporary (d. *c.*215), witnesses to their reception in the very different cultural and philosophical environment of that city. Clement's surviving trilogy of writings contains an apologetic *Exhortation* (*Protreptikos*), *The Instructor* (*Paidagogos*)—catechetical instruction for those who would follow Christ the pedagogue, the one who leads us to God—and the lengthy books of 'Miscellanies' (*Stromateis*), unsystematic discussions of subtler Christian issues for those capable of advancing to the acquisition of 'true gnosis'.

Attention has often been given to Clement's interest in resonances of Christian belief in Greek literature and philosophy, as well as his belief in a higher knowledge not available to all. It is increasingly clear, however, that he is combating the same opponents as Irenaeus. Thus he teaches that there is no elaborate spiritual *pleroma*, but one divine creator whose Son came in the flesh. There is only one divine economy of salvation embracing both covenants in a lengthy process of overcoming the passions that impede the perfection of the soul. The 'true gnosis' to which not all can aspire does not belong to some élite group of those who are 'spiritual by nature'. Baptism, not knowledge, is the basis of salvation (*Paed.* 2. 6. 25): and true Christian teaching at every level is based on reading the scriptures in conformity with the 'rule of faith' or 'ecclesiastical rule' (e.g. *Strom.* 6. 15. 124–5).

While he is indebted to Irenaeus at many points, Clement is critical of him as well, as in the rejection of the notion that body as well as soul partakes of the divine image (*Strom.* 2. 19. 3. 102). Moreover he recasts Irenaean themes to fit his own presuppositions. The classical theme of *paedeia*, the education of the soul towards full life, is seen in his reworking of the Irenaean dictum regarding the Incarnation: Irenaeus' 'the divine became human so that the human may become divine' becomes 'the divine became human so that humanity might learn, from a human being, how to become divine' (*Prot.* 1. 8. 4). On the other hand, while Clement opposes the detailed schemes of his Gnostic opponents, he can sympathize with the philosophical concern with human perfection which he finds particularly in the Valentinians. In him we see the now generally received principle of interpreting the scriptures according to the 'rule of faith' as it functions amidst the issues and interests of the intellectual world of Alexandria.

Origen's career began at Alexandria in the generation after Clement. He left c.230 for Caesarea Maritima in Palestine and died in 254. Unquestionably the pivotal Greek Christian theologian of the first half of the 3rd century, his controversial teaching absorbed attention long after his death. The preface to his *On First Principles* immediately reveals the similarities and differences between Origen's and earlier understandings of Christian thought. The apostles delivered certain key teachings in the plainest terms to all believers, but left it to those to whom 'the Holy Spirit gave gifts of language, wisdom, and knowledge' to consider the grounds for these doctrines, and set aside other matters for examination by those with the capacity for it (*praef.* 3). For these key teachings he quotes a threefold baptismal confession of faith (probably that of his Alexandrian congregation), but points out questions left unanswered and matters requiring further consideration.

The preface is crucial: the two major sections of the work (1. 1–2. 3; 2. 4–4. 3) follow this outline, as does the 'recapitulation' (4. 4). From a basic confession of faith issues of scriptural interpretation are approached, but with a profoundly intellectual cast. The apostolic teachings are rational propositions, and the discovery of their basis and investigation of further matters requires deeper intellectual insight. It is assumed that the divine revelation is in the words of the scriptures themselves—of both the 'old' and the 'new' covenants—to be appropriated according to the abilities of the believer. Alexandria's intellectual milieu is clearly visible.

Two subjects preoccupy Origen throughout his writing. His exegetical principles force him to deal with the status of the Son, the divine Word or Wisdom. While only the Father is unbegotten, the spiritual Word or Wisdom is beyond temporality and materiality and thus 'eternally begotten' (1. 2; 4. 4. 1). Hence the Word or Wisdom, and the Holy Spirit, are not assimilated to created things (1. 3. 7–8; 4. 4. 1). On the problem of evil, Origen, like Irenaeus, ascribes the turning of rational creatures from God to human freedom. He finds, at the spiritual level of scripture, an account of a multitude of pre-existing rational souls turning in varying degrees from God through 'satiety' (*koros*). The present form of embodied existence has been given to them as a place of training and education. The purpose of the divine economy of salvation is the return of all rational creatures to their original state at the 'consummation of all things' (*apokatastasis*) (1. 5–2. 3; 2. 10. 3–6). The incarnation of the Word or Wisdom, in whose image all are created, is the turning-point in the process. In both these subjects, Origen is addressing problems not dealt with before but now seen to be unavoidable; his solutions, however, include difficulties which are also part of his legacy.

The latter part of the 3rd century saw further attempts of the Roman government to destroy the Christian movement, before giving way under Constantine and Licinius to the first stage (313) in the reversal of policy.

The most visible effect of the persecutions on the development of Christian thought is in the Latin west. In the face of widespread apostasy during the persecution of Decius (248–50), and subsequent repentance on the part of apostates, the question of the pure church, a preoccupation of Tertullian, took concrete form in the episcopacy of Cyprian of Carthage (d. 258). With the support of Cornelius, bishop of Rome, Cyprian was willing to restore those who had not actually performed sacrifices. He was confronted with a schism begun by bishop Novatian, whose followers considered that such restorations revealed Cyprian and his associates as having forfeited any claim to true Christian commitment or to being Christians at all. Cyprian's rejoinder, *On the Unity of the Catholic Church* (*De unitate catholicae ecclesiae*), was that breaking communion with the authentic episcopal succession was the greater danger to Christian existence (6, 19). This view in turn would be used in 311 by supporters of bishop Donatus to argue that bishops who handed over books and vessels in the final persecution had proved themselves unfit to be called the authentic episcopate as defined by Cyprian and confirmed by his martyr's death. Latin Africa was to wrestle through the 4th century with the issues raised in the Donatist schism.

The Greek Christian world also faced the issue of apostasy, but was perhaps more open to understanding the mixed motives of the apostates, as witness the *Canonical Letter* of bishop Peter of Alexandria (martyred 311). But, as regards the east, interest must centre on the variety of reactions to the work of Origen. While the *Apology for Origen* (*Apologia pro Origene*) of Pamphilus (martyred *c.*310), in co-operation with Eusebius of Caesarea (d. *c.*340), defends Origen's scriptural work, underlining the speculative character of disputed aspects of his thought, Methodius of Olympus (martyred *c.*310), besides rejecting what he construed as Origen's insufficient commitment to the resurrection of bodies, interpreted his speculations regarding the generation of the cosmos as equivalent to declaring it a second uncreated being (*Creat.* 2–7).

Concluding reflections

The figures of this period should not be seen simply as foreshadowing later issues which they may have anticipated, left to be treated, or provoked. Looked at in themselves, their basic achievement was a rough consensus—so widely accepted as to go largely unrecognized today—regarding Christian thought as the interpretation of the emerging body of Christian scriptures in the light of the baptismal 'rule of faith'. The diverse issues which were taken up in pursuing this task—the relation of God and creation, the status of the Son, Word, or Wisdom, the purpose of the incarnation, the destiny of human embodiment—arose against the background of the challenge of Gnosticism, of issues in current philosophical discussion, and, inevitably, of differences between Christians themselves.

Intersecting these issues, however, and providing their ultimate context, is the assumption that the divine plan of salvation is now entering its final phase with the coming of Christ and the gift of the Spirit. This is arguably the fundamental context of Christian thought from the earliest Christian writings, where the proclamation of Jesus as Messiah requires a rethinking of Israel's interpretations of the past and expectations of the future. It is this question of the plan of salvation that underlies Justin's explanation of Christianity as the historical fulfilment of the Jewish scriptural promises; which is the basic issue between Irenaeus and his Valentinians; is restated by Tertullian in the light of Roman assumptions about the divine control of history; is rethought in Clement's Christian *paedeia*; and is the source of the problems that Origen sought to resolve through his grand vision of the fall and restoration of souls. Nor would this assumption be lost in the seemingly more dogmatic debates of the period to come.

PRIMARY SOURCES: the largest English translation series is the *Ante-Nicene Fathers* (1886), repr. (1994). Wherever possible, translations in the *Ancient Christian Writers* and *Fathers of the Church* series should be used. J. Stevenson, *A New Eusebius*, 2nd edn. (1985), is a useful source book.

Campenhausen, H. von, *The Formation of the Christian Bible* (1972).
Chadwick, H., *Early Christian Thought and the Classical Tradition* (1966).
Crouzel, H., *Origen: The Life and Thought of the First Great Theologian*, ET (1989).
Daley, B. E., *The Hope of the Early Church* (1991).
Evans, R. F., *One and Holy: the Church in Latin Christian Thought* (1972).
Ferguson, E. (ed.), 'Orthodoxy, Heresy, and Schism in Early Christianity', *Studies in Early Christianity*, 4 (1993).
Gonzalez, J., *History of Christian Thought*, 2nd edn. (1988), i.
Grant, R. M., *Gods and the One God* (1986).
—— *The Greek Apologists of the Second Century* (1988).
Hinchcliff, P., *Cyprian of Carthage and the Unity of the Christian Church* (1974).
Jefford, C. N., *Reading the Apostolic Fathers* (1996).
Kelly, J. N. D., *Early Christian Creeds*, 3rd edn. (1972).
Lilla, S. A. C., *Clement of Alexandria: A Study in Christian Platonism and Gnosticism* (1971).
Norris, R. A., *God and World in Early Christian Theology* (1965).
—— 'The Transcendence and Freedom of God in Irenaeus', in W. R. Schoedel and R. L. Wilken (eds.), *Early Christian Literature and the Classical Intellectual Tradition* (1979).
—— 'Theology and Language in Irenaeus of Lyons', *Anglican Theological Review*, 74 (1994).

Orbe, A., *Antropologia de San Ireneo* (1969).

Patterson, L. G., *Methodius of Olympus* (1997).

—— 'The Divine Became Human: Irenaean Themes in Clement of Alexandria', *Studia Patristica*, 31 (1997).

Proctor, E., *Christian Controversy in Alexandria: Clement's Polemic Against Basilideans and Valentinians* (1995).

Trigg, J. W., *Origen: The Bible and Philosophy in the Third Century Church* (1983).

van den Hoek, A., *Clement of Alexandria and his Use of Philo in the Stromateis* (1988).

Vivian, T., *St. Peter of Alexandria: Bishop and Martyr* (1988).

Wilken, R. L., *The Christians as the Romans Saw Them* (1984).

CHRISTIAN THOUGHT IN THE EAST

II

CONTROVERSY AND COUNCILS
Greek theology, 4th–6th centuries

John McGuckin

THE GREEK-SPEAKING CHRISTIAN WORLD BETWEEN THE 4th and 6th centuries experienced one of the most vital periods in the history of Christian theology, experiencing factions and conflicts, both political and intellectual, which at times threatened the church's coherent long-term survival. The intellectual demands made upon Christian thinkers of that period, however, led to the adoption and development of basic positions that would characterize Christianity for many centuries. This can be seen both in the intellectual methods of argument adopted to resolve difficulties, and in those structural forms of organization and procedure the church came to favour. Many of the foundations of these positions had been laid down in the cultural movement from Semitic to more overtly Greek forms of thought and expression that accelerated throughout the church of the 2nd and 3rd centuries. It is in the period under consideration, however, that we see refined and tested centrally important understandings of the nature of God and God's involvement with the world; the dynamic significance of the person and work of Jesus; the concept of Trinity; the ways deemed appropriate of reading the scriptural foundations of Christian thought; the forms of the churches' liturgical and sacramental life; and the infrastructures of Christian local and global ecclesiastical organization. Many of these matters were not to be thought about seriously again,

or challenged in their essential structure, until the late Middle
Ages.

🌿 Exegetical foundations

Much of the pattern for 4th-century Christian thought had been
laid down by Origen of Alexandria. Even his enemies could not
ignore him. His metaphysical speculations were increasingly
downplayed in subsequent centuries, but he determined the
agenda in terms of the doctrine of Christ's salvific work and
his relation to the divine absolute for almost all the leading
thinkers of the 4th century. The chief intellectual issue driving
the whole of Origen's time, and much of the century following,
was the problematic relation of the absolute God to a contingent
world. Several of the Hellenistic schools, especially the Stoics,
Middle-Platonists, and Neo-Pythagoreans, had challenged Christians to think out more fully the metaphysical and cosmological
implications of theology that were so notably absent from their
biblical accounts. Origen had responded by focusing his thought
on the crucial issue of the relation of the One to the Many, and by
positing Christ, both as the eternal Word (Logos) and the histor-
ically realized teacher Jesus, as supreme mediator between the
worlds. The refining of this cosmic christology became the master
theme of 4th-century thought. To illustrate the mediating role of
the Logos made flesh, Origen systematized a method of interpreting the scriptures that allowed eternal meaning to be drawn from
apparently relativized historical texts, by a manner of allegorical
and typological (spiritualized) readings. The approach was enthusiastically adopted by the church of the next century, and greatly
simplified in the process. The great change from a 3rd- to a 4th-
century context, however, can be seen in the different manners of
approaching the result of those exegeses. Many times, where Origen speaks tentatively and speculatively (addressing a circle of
scholars and disciples), the 4th-century theologians wished to
proceed to a more definite expression of truth. The methods
appropriate to the small groups of advanced readers for whom

Origen wrote had given way to a universalized doctrine meant for a greater mass of hearers in the churches. The age of doctrinal formulation had arrived with a flourish, and was advanced by key figures and teachers who wove together in their biblical expositions the insights they had gained from extensive classical rhetorical educations. The introduction, in this period, of philosophical key terms to elucidate theological arguments is very noticeable. The pace of the intellectual exchange in the 4th century was undoubtedly fuelled also by the extraordinary opportunities afforded to Christians after their emergence from a long period of political disapproval, if not active persecution, into the (relative) sunlight of the Constantinian dynasty.

Christological disputes

The 4th century was a period of great conflicts and internal confusions among Christian teachers, centred round the two primary disputes over christological and Trinitarian theology. Both issues were rooted in the ways that different schools approached scriptural exegesis. In the early part of the 4th century the Arian controversy over the status of Christ had found opposing parties appealing for contradictory conclusions to the selfsame body of texts. If such a massive conflict in basic conclusions was all too obvious, how could the church ever deduce coherent doctrine from such a disparate collection as its biblical canon? The controversies of this era were equally issues of how to nuance the fundamental problem of addressing the manner in which the Absolute God approached a contingent world, and thus almost all the disputes that racked the 4th-century church can be seen as the working out of the corollaries of Logos theology.

Here again the legacy of Origen, who had taught both the pre-temporal origination of the Logos, and his subordination to the supreme God, was central. This question of how a mediating Logos could itself be an absolute had been tormenting the church in the early decades of the 4th century. Though the idea first came to prominence in Alexandria where a forceful hierarch had anathematized the presbyter Arius for his subordinationist theology, many parties now perceived these twin aspects of Origen's system to be contradictory, and threatening to disrupt the coherence of the larger communion of churches in the east. The Arian crisis ran far beyond the issues raised by Arius and his bishop Alexander, but his case had already divided the eastern church for several years before Constantine called an international synod at Nicaea in 325, to settle the christological dispute (as he hoped) once and for all. Athanasius had been a young deacon then, but he inherited the see of Alexandria shortly afterwards and propagated a hardline defence of Nicene christology as the only authentic inheritor of the biblical and apostolic faith. At the outset he regarded the party-word 'consubstantial' (the Logos was *homoousios*, that is of the same essence of God, and thus truly God in every significant nuance of that title) as a dispensable factor if the sense was agreed (it was controversial to many because it was not a biblical designation), but as synod succeeded synod throughout the first half of the 4th century, factionalizing the churches, he soon came to realize that attachment to the word (bringing with it the support of western Christians) would be a useful policy, both to simplify the debate and offer a rallying-point of unity. Athanasius' own understanding of the christology of *homoousios* was soteriologically led; he saw the descent of the Logos to earth as an act of the redemption and re-creation of fallen creatures. As God became human, he argued, so humans might become divine. The Incarnation was a deification of the body of the Logos, and thereby an archetypal pattern for the deification of all humanity by grace. Athanasius saw the cosmic battles fought in the sacred body of Jesus, for example the fight with, and conquering of, death in the flesh, as an ontological victory for all humankind. Only later in his life did some of the negative implications of such a powerful 'divine-agent christology' become apparent. Because of the context of his apologetic, Athanasius was thought by several of his contemporaries (and most modern commentators) not to have laid sufficient emphasis on the human soul of Jesus. More fundamentally, Christian thinkers of the generation after Athanasius began to worry about the whole rationale of a consubstantial christology, just at the moment its future seemed secure—at the very end of the 4th century when the Emperor Theodosius I positively proscribed Arianism at the Council of Constantinople in 381 and held up Nicene orthodoxy as the future standard for the Christian empire.

The theologians of the generation after Athanasius, who subscribed to the Nicene tradition, were faced with a great dilemma: if Christ was as coequally absolute as the Father, had not the whole point and purpose of a Logos christology (wherein the Logos functions as a subordinate divine mediator between the realms of absolute and contingent) been thoroughly disrupted? It was a younger generation of Asia Minor thinkers who took his christological effort forward with significant adaptations, the Neo-Nicenes, pre-eminent among whom was a circle of friends and relations: Basil of Caesarea (330–79), his brother Gregory of Nyssa (c.331/40–395), and the learned Gregory Nazianzen (c.329–90). Together with the latter's cousin, Amphilokius, and Basil's ascetic sister Macrina, these are collectively known as the Cappadocians. The bishop theologians among them were stimulated to their argument by the late and radical school of anti-Nicene theology known as Neo-Arianism, or Eunomianism.

In the 350s and 360s the dialectician Aetius, aided by his devoted pupil Eunomius, had emerged as a rallying-point for all radical opposition to the various Nicene parties and the Homoiousians, those parties willing to go halfway towards the Nicene position merely stating the Son's fundamental likeness to the Father, though without having necessarily to elaborate a Trinitarian theology, or disrupt the principle of having only one absolute divine person. Taking their cue from the majority Arian faction known as the Homoians (who argued that the Son was simply 'like the Father') whom they regarded as time-serving compromisers, the Neo-Arians elaborated a theology of the Son's radical 'unlikeness' to God (hence they were named Anomoians). In 359 Aetius proposed a dense, syllogistical synopsis of theology, his *Syntagmation*. He argued that the scriptural texts reveal God

21

as fundamentally 'the Unbegotten Cause' of all. As the Son is defined by scripture to be begotten he is, therefore, caused, and thus no part of the Father, though related to him as a primary effect of the divine will. Although the Son issues from before time, he is a contingent part of creation. Eunomius, after his teacher's death, was to press forward this theology with even greater stress on the revelatory force of names and titles in scripture. The latter further argued that correctness in doctrine was not merely an essential prerequisite for holiness, but was itself constitutive of holiness. The sharply dialectical method of the school, and its logical development to a view of God who was perfectly self-revelatory, and logically consistent, led many to hold them in disdain. Their premisses brought about many of the characteristic traits of the Cappadocian theologians who opposed them, in particular their stress on two fundamental insights opposed to the Neo-Arians: first that the scriptural titles possessed merely a dynamic force— that is when names such as Father and Son are used in scripture they function as suggestive analogies rather than absolute revelants (and so an authentic method of scriptural exegesis has to be contextually sensitive and multivalent); and secondly, over and against Aetius' view of a perfectly cogent self-revealing God, that God was essentially incomprehensible, and obscure even in his acts of revelation. The net result of the Cappadocian theology was to raise a severe warning about the limits of systematic reason in the face of the nature and person of God, and this was to set a dominant tone for centuries of eastern Christian theology to come.

This defence of christology left the Cappadocians with the difficulty of explaining how one knew, at any given instance, whether a scriptural text carried the full weight of a metaphysical revelation about the nature of God, or was merely an illustrative analogy; whether it referred to the ideal world or the contingent; whether it described God in himself, or simply evoked God in his dealings with the world: to meet this problem they argued that the role of the interpreter was critical. Such a man (presumed to be an educated and ascetically purified bishop) would have been tested and refined in the rigours of spiritual *askesis* so that all arbitrary and sense-bound elements of his mind would have been clarified. He would thus be an archetypal teacher of the truth in line with the ancient gospel tradition. This stress on the purified nature of the true interpreter was the main subtext of the massively influential *Five Theological Orations* by Gregory Nazianzen (*Orations*, 27–31), which he delivered at Constantinople in 380 as a synopsis of the Neo-Nicene faith in God as Trinity. It was meant to (and did) become a standard synopsis of orthodox theology for subsequent generations.

The stress on the purified interpreter might seem curiously individualistic for a church emerging from a generation of crises caused by conflicts of schools, but it signalled the lack of faith in the solution proposed in the early 4th century: synodical consensus as a guide to truth. During the main era of the Arian crisis so many councils had been held, mutually anathematizing each other, that any belief in the usefulness of this method for identifying and promulgating authentic Christian tradition had been severely shaken. In the aftermath of the Council of Constantinople (381) Gregory Nazianzen dismissed the whole affair as 'quacking geese' and concluded that 'nothing good' could ever come from such meetings. The Cappadocians, setting asceticism as a necessary prelude for theological accuracy, tried to restrict the development of theological speculation considered as a philosophical quest. In this they largely succeeded. Monastic ascetical communities would serve henceforth as a fostering community for theologians, and would check their philosophically speculative range.

The Cappadocian era is especially notable for its contribution to the theology of Trinity. Augustine would contribute a large element of the picture later, in his *De Trinitate*, but his influence would extend only over the west. In the eastern church the Cappadocians were the unchallenged masters of this fundamental Christian teaching. Among them Gregory Nazianzen is the most explicit. God, he says, is to be acknowledged as being one in nature, and three in hypostasis. The three hypostases (persons,

23

or subsistent entities) are each possessed of the same nature (or being). The diversity appears in the manner in which the contingent world experiences the unapproachable God. God is unapproachable in his essence, but reaches out to the created world by means of his hypostases. Thus, the Father who 'begets' the Logos, and 'sends out' the Holy Spirit is the solitary cause of the Trinity. This justifies Christians claiming to believe in only one God. The Father's hypostatic existence is explained as the sole cause of the other two, and as such he is the ground of unity of the divine being. The Son and Spirit come in discrete ways from the one Father to express the divine power of outreach (thus although God is unknowable and unapproachable he also expresses himself as desiring to be known and approached) and to effect the salvation among earthly beings that will realize this revelation of the true God among them. For Gregory, as the hypostases of Son and Spirit share the single divine being of the Father, all three are coequal and coeternal, and yet the rationale of the threefold process of Trinity is assured by the inner logic of the Trinitarian dynamic movement. The Father, being sole cause of the other hypostases, effects the movement within the Godhead that results in the outreach to all creation. Yet the Father, understood as cause of all within the eternal life of Godhead, remains beyond all external movement that can be considered as contingent. God is thus the Unmoved Mover. The Trinity is fundamentally the outreach of its cause: that is the Father's dynamic concern to draw all creatures back to himself, through the Son, in the Spirit. In its original design and intent, therefore, Trinitarian theology was an essay in biblical soteriology as much as a metaphysical speculation on the nature of the relation of the divine to the cosmos.

The complexity of this doctrine, which became the capstone of a Christianity now able to explicate, to itself and to others, why it offered supreme veneration to Jesus, was to be an intellectual handicap in the hands of lesser minds than those as versed in bible and philosophy as the Cappadocians. This was especially true in the face of the advance of Islam in the eastern provinces from the 7th century onwards, where a radically simple doctrine of God was set in opposition to a difficult and nuanced Christian position. Nevertheless, the genius of the Cappadocian approach was that it managed, finally, to resolve the problems of the relative status of the divine Logos and the Spirit, and to affirm clearly that Christians worship Jesus as God without idolatrously elevating a man to divine honours. It also served to reconcile a doctrine of an absolute God with the biblical sense of a God who loves and cares for a people of his own in a highly involved relationship. In a real sense, the Cappadocian doctrine of Trinity created from the forge of two centuries of bitter Christian controversies a final synthesis of the Judaic and Hellenistic insights into theology: the God who acts in history, and the God who is beyond all movement. Even though, after the 4th century, it was hardly developed much again, theologians being content to repeat the formularies of the earlier writers, the concept of Trinity was dynamically maintained in the doxologies and prayers of the eastern church.

🌿 Liturgical developments

After Constantine came to power he dispensed large grants to the Christians, partly in compensation for properties confiscated. Several key building projects resulted, most notably the great new churches at Rome, Constantinople, and Jerusalem, which came to have a stimulating effect on the development of Christian liturgy and a reflective theology of the cult. At the Church of the Holy Sepulchre the various sites within the same complex—the tomb of Jesus, the Anastasis, the place of Calvary, and the baptismal pool—led to a style of ceremonial which, together with that of the imperial capital in later centuries, would prove highly influential. There survives from one of the bishops of the Jerusalem Church in the 4th century a set of liturgical homilies, or Catecheses. Their author, Cyril of Jerusalem (d. 387), was a leading protagonist in the Arian struggles, whose sympathies at various times both Nicenes and anti-Nicenes thought they could command. He delivered his Catecheses through Lent for the benefit of candidates for baptism. He is also the probable author of a series of lectures on the sacraments. In these works Cyril presents the Christian rituals as awesome mysteries, and lays down the basis for a more solemn structuring of the liturgical life of the church than had been previously witnessed. From his time onwards the liturgy was to grow in magnificence, and his association of ritual and sacramental meaning was to be immensely influential in the establishment of an enduring liturgical theology.

✄ Graeco-Syrian influences on the east-Christian tradition

Close neighbours to the north, the Syrian Church's literature had from earliest times been marked by ascetical interests. Writers such as Aphrahat and Ephrem (c.306–73) had laid down a body of literature that was rich with biblical symbols, hymnal and rhapsodic in character. They worked out a theology less apologetically driven than their Greek-speaking neighbours, and more explicitly concerned with the great themes of an ascetical return to paradisal bliss. By the end of the 4th century, this Syrian tradition was at home in the literature of the Greeks, though it was never to lose its sensitivity to the local traditions and traits that had made Syrian thought distinctive. At this period it produced a great school of exegesis, in Syriac and Greek, with such luminaries as Diodore of Tarsus (d. c.390), his younger contemporaries and disciples Theodore of Mopsuestia (c.350–428) and John Chrysostom (c.347–407) (the latter becoming one of the most influential models of 'Greek' Christian rhetoric), and, in the early 5th century, Nestorius and Theodoret of Cyrrhus (c.393–457) who were to witness a massive attack launched on their traditions of christology by Cyril of Alexandria (c.375–444), a barrage that would be responsible for the posthumous synodical condemnation in 553, under the emperor Justinian, of the leading Antiochene teachers.

The Syrian tradition influenced the Greek world mainly through its approach to scripture, which adopted a critical distance from much of what Origen had recommended. Lucian of Antioch (d. 312) founded a school of interpretation that, much more markedly than the Alexandrians (who preferred a transcendental exegesis of the texts), was more carefully attentive to the social and historical significance. Lucian drew a devoted circle of admirers round him. His edition of the Septuagint became the standard text received in all the churches of the east, and his edition of the NT is the foundation of what is now the *Textus Receptus*. Lucian's biblical method was taken forward by Diodore of Tarsus. In his time Diodore was one of the leading Christian opponents to the emperor Julian's policy for the revival of paganism, and worked tirelessly to produce philosophically sensitive treatises attacking the anti-Christian factions of his day. He founded a monastery and school near Antioch and was there the teacher of Theodore Mopsuestia and John Chrysostom, who spread the exegetical traditions to Constantinople and throughout the east, after their elections as bishops. Diodore's approach to the biblical text deliberately undermined the readings preferred by Origen. He followed a consistently historical reading, from which he wished to demonstrate higher significances. Allegorical interpretation, he argued, abused the literal sense and therefore could not rise to a higher veracity. In his treatment of the Blessings of Jacob, or the first fifty Psalms, on which he comments, it is noticeable how only those passages are accepted as 'messianic' that traditional Jewish exegesis had already accepted as such. This amounted to a very few texts indeed (in this case only Gen. 49: 10–12; and Pss. 2, 8, and 44). This was in stark contrast to the general tendencies already witnessed in the mainstream of Christian interpretation that gave messianic readings to a much larger body of biblical loci. The practical results can be seen most visibly in his christology. He was an avowed opponent of Apollinaris (*c*.315–92), his opposite pole, who taught that Jesus was a divine being inhabiting a veil of flesh, not needing to commit himself to a fully human life in so far as his divine power absorbed and 'included in' anything necessary for a visitation of humankind on earth. Diodore held any form of monist christology such as this in horror. He urged, rightly, that it presented the death of incarnation theology in favour of an epiphanic theology of Jesus that was more akin to earlier Docetic thought, where Jesus' real status as a human being was undermined. Yet, as a result of his apologetic intent, his language often seemed to others outside his school to be too heavily dualist. He spoke of christology in terms of 'Two Sons': one Son before the ages, the other a Son within time. It was a language that was to lie behind much of his disciples' work, and even lasted into the 5th century, providing the backdrop to Nestorius' bitter opposition to Cyril.

Theodore Mopsuestia was, in the late 4th century, an eminent practitioner of the methods of Diodore. He was regarded in his own time as the leading Syrian theologian, but his reputation was fatally damaged in the aftermath of the 5th-century christological controversy and finally he was posthumously condemned in 553 when Justinian's council anathematized him as a 'forebear' of the heresy of 'Nestorianism'. Theodore's biblical commentaries were firmly focused on the literal reading, and he only lightly touched on the issue of the NT as a typological fulfilment of the OT. Instead he stressed that the individual Christian believer looks to his type in Christ. Part of the reason for this is that he has a firm doctrine of successive ages of revelation: the first given to the pagans, the second to the Jews, the last to the Christians. The NT stands only partly in relation to the OT. It complements it, but does not unerringly fulfil it, since it often supersedes it, and thus its meaning cannot be explicated out of the OT text, as if both were a seamless robe in the manner Origen had looked on them. Through Chrysostom's work which popularized many of these approaches, though in a less radical form, and which became staple reading in the East, the Syrian influence came home to have a permanent impact on Greek Christian thought.

✳ The 5th-century controversies

Throughout the 4th century Christian asceticism had been growing in extent. The classic forms of desert monasticism had already been subjected to much variation as communities grew up in the cities and villages. Monasticism, at first a wilderness experience often at odds with hierarchical authority, had become urbanized, and ascetic teachers were more and more sought out as bishops of important cities. By the 5th century a pattern of theological process that is rooted in *askesis* and looks to past precedent for its doctrinal formulations becomes clearly observable. Now, it is the nexus of monastic parties and communities that does much to determine the successful outcome of great intellectual issues. By the 5th century the appeal to scripture had evolved into a procedure that wished to amass as many proof-texts as possible. In this era one can also see that system extended from the scriptures as authoritative sources and into the works of theologians from earlier generations who have now come to be seen as standard-bearers of orthodoxy, and to whom is given the title 'Abbas' or 'fathers'. This century is the age, properly speaking, of 'patristic' theology. Nowhere are the issues more clearly seen than in the greatest of the controversies of the 5th century, the christological dispute that flared up between the great sees of Alexandria and Constantinople in the persons of their respective archbishops Cyril and Nestorius. It was a dispute that was to constitute the agenda for all the christological debates of the 6th century too.

Whereas Nestorius argued that christology ought to be marked above all else by clarity of thought and language, Cyril appealed to the essential 'mystery' of the Christ event (and consequent necessary mysteriousness of theology). Above all, Cyril called on a whole dossier of patristic authorities which he had his chancery scribes assemble. This method in theological argumentation, the compiling of the patristic authorities who support one's opinion about scriptural exegesis and dogmatic formulary, became the standard form of Christian theological method from this time until the medieval scholastic period. It can be first seen in its full legal and scholastic process in the procedural documentation of the Council of Ephesus 431. The christological solution proposed at Ephesus made Alexandrian premisses the chief starting-point for reflection on the role of Jesus. But what the Syrian and Western churches thought to be an excessive monism in the Alexandrian pattern of thought ensured that the conflict would occupy much of the 5th and 6th centuries, in a string of imperially sponsored councils and decrees. The decision of the Council of Ephesus, affirming that Jesus the Christ was a single and coherent divine person inhominated, was further extrapolated at the Council of Chalcedon (because of Syrian and Roman pressures) to affirm that this single person was also endowed with two complete natures (divine and human) united under a single personhood (hypostasis). This came to be known as hypostatic christology and was adopted as the standard of orthodoxy by most of the churches.

✣ Sixth-century conflict and resolutions

Many of the Alexandrian school of theologians thought that the Syrian-influenced stress on the duality of natures in Christ had strayed into a revival of Diodore's excessive dualism. In the semantics of the time there was a fine line between the notion of person and that of nature, and the Greek terms used in the debate contributed to the confusion. Many thought that Chalcedon was propounding a hopelessly artificial view of Christ. Several important theologians in Egypt and Syria began a protest movement against the council and its doctrine of two natures (Dyophysitism). They came, therefore, to be known as the Monophysites.

Severus of Antioch (c.465–538) was perhaps the greatest intellectual among them. Their main points were taken from the works of Cyril of Alexandria, and were meant to advance a mystically coherent vision of Jesus as a divine being who had deified the flesh that he had assumed. They attempted to rehabilitate the transcendent aspects of Alexandrian christology while avoiding the defects of Apollinaris. The arguments that ensued over fine points of christology radically disrupted the peace of the eastern Christian world at every level. Monasteries were almost at war with each other throughout Palestine, and in Egypt and Syria the cohesion of the hierarchies was substantially damaged. Imperial efforts to enforce agreement, under one or another emperor, were sometimes subtle and sometimes heavy-handed throughout the 5th and 6th centuries. In 544 the court of Justinian issued an explicit condemnation of the dualistic christology of three of the leading Syrian authorities: Theodore, Theodoret, and Ibas of Edessa, in an attempt to appease and reconcile the Monophysite party. This edict, known as the Three Chapters, was reaffirmed at the imperially sponsored Council of Constantinople II in 553. This too attempted a reconciliation between the Dyophysite and Monophysite factions on the basis of a more nuanced interpretation of Chalcedon. It was an effort that was largely in vain. The social effects of the ecclesiastical divisions in the east were finally resolved only when the most troublesome provinces of Syria and Egypt were lost to imperial control in the Arab advances of the 7th century. The theological differences have remained to this day as the leading cause of division among eastern Christians, and comparable, as far as they are concerned, to the fractures consequent on the Reformation controversies later in the west.

As the 6th century drew to a close, in an eastern empire that was increasingly stretched to preserve its political integrity and fiscal sufficiency, a highly influential figure was born, who in many ways was a precursor of times to come. Maximus the Confessor (580–662) was destined to be the great representative link between the late antique period and the flourishing of Byzantine theological thought in the centuries ahead, in the east. For all his brilliance, however, and the cosmic range and character of his speculative intelligence, he is to all intents and purposes a great systematizer of what has gone before. He is a commentator, a scholiast, an explicator, and in this represents the slowing down, if not the closure, of a great era of active and frequently disruptive theological debate in the east Christian world. After him the world of late antiquity is definitively over and early medieval Byzantium beckons.

Barnes, T. D., *Athanasius and Constantius: Theology and Politics in the Constantinian Empire* (1994).

Frend, W. H. C., *The Rise of the Monophysite Movement* (1972).

—— *The Rise of Christianity* (1984).

Grillmeier, A., *Christ in Christian Tradition*, 2nd edn. (1975), i.

Hanson, R. P. C., *The Search for the Christian Doctrine of God* (1988).

Kelly, J. N. D., *Early Christian Doctrines* (1958).

McGuckin, J. A., *St. Cyril of Alexandria: The Christological Controversy* (1994).

Meyendorff, J., *Byzantine Theology* (1975).

—— *Imperial Unity and Christian Divisions* (1989).

Norris, R. A., *Manhood and Christ: A Study in the Christology of Theodore Mopsuestia* (1963).

Pelikan, J., *The Christian Tradition*, i. *The Emergence of the Classical Tradition* (1974).

—— *Christianity and Classical Culture* (1993).

Rousseau, P., *Basil of Caesarea* (1994).

Simonetti, M., *Biblical Exegesis in the Early Church* (1994).

Young, F., *From Nicaea to Chalcedon* (1983).

Zaharopoulos, D. Z., *Theodore of Mopsuestia on the Bible* (1989).

III

CREATION AND ASCETISM
Syriac Christian thought

Susan Ashbrook Harvey

SYRIAC IS A DIALECT OF ARAMAIC ORIGINATING IN THE region of Edessa, now the city of Urfa in south-eastern Turkey. In the early Christian era, it emerged as the lingua franca over a wide area of the eastern Roman empire, the Persian empire, and beyond. It remains a living language among Christian communities in what is now Syria, Lebanon, south-eastern Turkey, Israel, Iraq, and Iran, and a liturgical language for a sizeable Christian population in south India. Its greatest theological writings were produced between the 4th and 7th centuries, followed by an extraordinary flowering of mysticism between the 7th and 10th centuries. Western Christians have tended to interpret Christian history through the paradigms of Greek east and Latin west. Syriac Christianity represents a third Christian tradition, one equally ancient but one whose expressions and experiences do not fit those familiar in the west.

Syriac Christian thought found much of its finest articulation in the poetic works of such writers as Ephrem of Nisibis ('the Harp of the Holy Spirit', d. 373), a poet without peer in any Christian language for many centuries, Narsai (d. 502), and Jacob of Serug ('the Flute of the Holy Spirit', d. 521). Whether hymns, verse homilies, or rhythmic prose, poetry was often the favoured mode of religious reflection for Syriac writers, where Greek and Latin patristic thinkers chose philosophical treatises of a more analytical nature. In the elusive and allusive wordplay of poetry, the startling insights of metaphor, paradox, and symbol, Syriac writers sought to glimpse the divine rather than to define or limit its meaning. From the earliest Syriac texts through the great mystics, one finds a distinctive and powerful understanding of the Holy Spirit. Because the Syriac term for spirit, *ruha*, is grammatically feminine (as the Hebrew, *ruah*), early Syriac writers generally treated the Holy Spirit as feminine just as they referred to God and Christ in the masculine. Where Greek and Latin writers occasionally employed gendered images when speaking of the divine, in early Syriac texts the understanding of the Holy Spirit as feminine, based within the linguistic structure of the language itself, led to substantive theological developments. However, while no reference to the change survives, after 400 the Spirit in Syriac literature appears almost exclusively in masculine terms. The change occurred in the post-Nicene era when the church throughout its geographical expanse sought greater conformity in doctrinal language and practice. Perhaps the earlier Syriac tradition seemed too discordant in such a climate—a haunting constraint upon the diversity of ancient Christian spirituality.

Yet the Holy Spirit in Syriac thought continued to provide the activity most vividly linking Christian devotional practice with liturgical action and biblical event, an interplay stressed throughout Syriac literature. Thus one finds Syriac writers using the same lexical terms to indicate the action of the Holy Spirit over the waters of creation, upon Mary at the Annunciation, upon Christ at the baptism in the Jordan, and upon the disciples at Pentecost; the same again upon the believer at baptism, upon the bread and wine at the *epiclesis* (consecration) of the Eucharist, and upon the heart of the faithful Christian in prayer.

The rich identification between bible, liturgy, and devotional life also underlies the most notorious aspect of Syriac Christianity, its pervasive and sometimes severe ascetical spirituality. Yet the extremes of Syrian asceticism are part of a larger spectrum, in which the individual believer portrayed in bodily actions a symbolism in accordance with that of Syriac poetic theology. From our earliest texts a basic ascetic orientation was expected of every believer: simplicity in food and clothing, celibacy or chastity in marriage, care for the poor and sick. By the 3rd century, there emerged a consecrated lay order, the Sons and Daughters of the Covenant (or Covenanters), who took vows of celibacy and poverty, and devoted themselves to the service of the church community under the direction of priests or bishops; they maintained a visible presence until at least the 10th century. When monasticism developed over the course of the 4th century as a separated location for devotional practice, in the Syriac realm it did so in close interaction with town and village parishes, and churches in cities. As the 4th-century Syriac writer Aphrahat admonished, care for the sick and poor was also a practice of prayer—a practice without which prayer was not truly offered.

Syriac ascetic tradition is striking for the tireless immersion of its monks and nuns in service to the poor, oppressed, sick, and suffering of their day. As Christ had done, so too the ascetic battled hunger and weariness in the body through such disciplines as fasting and vigils, while ministry to the poor and sick fought against the suffering and injustice of the fallen world. The body both individual and collective could be forged anew, healed, and restored as Christ's own body in its resurrected reality. In the pure prayer taught by the mystics, the body of the ascetic became the church sanctuary, the heart the altar, the tears the incense offered upon the altar. The ascetic body and the ecclesial body could be seen to be one and the same.

The powerfully imagistic theological and ascetic traditions of Syriac Christianity drew upon the metaphorical possibilities of language and behaviour. Both expressions relied upon a sense that divine and human realms are interactive, that spiritual and physical realms are not opposed or incompatible, but rather that human experience in the physical realm is permeated with divine presence and activity. Thus one finds a marked celebration of nature and creation by Syriac writers. In Syriac tradition, there are two books of scripture: the bible itself, and the natural world. Syriac writers delighted to seek God's presence in every nook and cranny of nature, to see God's mark engraved on every aspect of the created order. There was an ecological celebration that still astounds the reader's senses. Such a sensibility pervaded even the most severe of Syriac ascetic writings, and thus warns against any simplistic charge of dualistic tendencies. The physical mattered in Syriac Christianity in all its aspects: the body, its actions, the world we inhabit, both civic and natural. To understand its fallen state was also to heed the promise of redeemed existence.

Syriac Christianity is sometimes known for rejecting the theological developments of the Greek east and Latin west. In truth, the heated christological controversies of the 5th century led to a tragic splintering of Syriac Christianity into separate church families: the Church of the East ('Nestorians'), the Syrian Orthodox (Jacobites or 'Monophysites'), and the Antiochian Orthodox ('Melkites'), each of these families also subsequently dividing into further denominations. Western names for these churches have derogatorily implied heretical status. Yet modern scholarship and the efforts of ecumenism have demonstrated that these traditions grew out of serious christological debates, in which differences in theological terminology and discourse were wrongly interpreted. In the current context of fresh reconsideration, the different Syriac churches provide important correctives in the development of christological doctrine. A further legacy of the divisive theological battles of the 5th and 6th centuries can be seen in Syriac literature itself. From the 6th century onwards, Syriac writers increasingly conform their style, presentation, and terminology to the dictates of Greek philosophical and theological discourse. At their best, Syriac writers like Philoxenus of Mabbug (d. 523) and Isaac the Syrian (late 7th century) combined Semitic and Hellenic traditions to yield a vibrant synthesis. After the 7th century, an even more powerful influence was exerted with the development of Islam, and Christian Arabic in response. Yet Syriac Christian thought preserved its most characteristic aspects in the continuing richness of its liturgical traditions, as well as continuing devotion to the writings of its poets and mystics. Throughout its history, Syriac has been the language of a cultural or religious minority. The brilliance of its

Christian thought, produced above all in its first millennium, has been the expression of Christian peoples without the power of kingdoms or empires to further their cause.

Brock, S. P., 'Mary in Syriac Tradition', in A. Stacpoole (ed.), *Mary's Place in Christian Dialogue* (1982).
—— *The Syriac Fathers on Prayer and the Spiritual Life* (1987).
—— *The Luminous Eye: The Spiritual World Vision of Saint Ephrem the Syrian*, rev. edn. (1992).
Griffith, S. H., 'Asceticism in the Church of Syria: The Hermeneutics of Early Syrian Monasticism', in V. L. Wimbush and R. Valantasis (eds.), *Asceticism* (1995).
Harvey, S. A., 'Feminine Imagery for the Divine: The Holy Spirit, the Odes of Solomon, and Early Syriac Tradition', *St. Vladimir's Theological Quarterly*, 37 (1993).
Moffatt, S. H., *A History of Christianity in Asia*, i. *Beginnings to 1500* (1992).
Murray, R., *Symbols of Church and Kingdom: A Study in Early Syriac Tradition* (1975).
Nedungatt, G., 'The Covenanters of the Early Syriac-Speaking Church', *Orientalia Christiana Periodica*, 39 (1973).
Segal, J. B., *Edessa: The Blessed City* (1970).

IV

WISDOM, INNER AND OUTER
Byzantine theology, 6th–16th centuries

Andrew Louth

BYZANTINE THEOLOGY WAS SHAPED BY THREE distinct, though intertwined, traditions: the ascetic or monastic tradition, the developing dogmatic tradition (Trinitarian theology and, especially, christology), and a continuing philosophical tradition, mainly Platonic and Neoplatonic in complexion. The philosophical tradition, with its pagan roots, was often referred to, dismissively, as 'exterior' (*exothen*), a usage that goes back to the Cappadocian fathers; the complementary terminology of an 'interior' (*esothen*) tradition came later, and was claimed by the monks. The 6th century saw decisive developments in all these three traditions.

By the end of the 6th century a considerable body of monastic literature had developed: the assembling of the traditions of the fathers of the Egyptian desert was still taking place at the beginning of the century, though by this time the centre of gravity of Orthodox monasticism had moved to Palestine and Sinai, whence stems the single most influential Byzantine monastic treatise, the *Ladder of Divine Ascent*, written perhaps at the turn of the 6th/7th century by John, Abbot of St Catherine's Monastery, Sinai, whom tradition identifies as simply 'of the Ladder', *tou Klimakos*. This monastic tradition of ascetic wisdom was deeply indebted to the great 4th-century theorist of the Egyptian eremitical life, Evagrius, himself much influenced by Origen; it owed no less a debt to the experiential tradition of the Macarian

Homilies. Origenism had been anathematized at Justinian's instigation in the 6th century—by imperial edict in 543 and at the Fifth Ecumenical Council in 553—but nonetheless it continued to appeal to many in monastic circles.

The dogmatic tradition also emerged from the 6th century with distinctive features. The Council of Chalcedon (451) had deeply divided Christians in the eastern provinces, and though Justinian's attempts at bridge-building failed, he marked forever the Byzantine dogmatic tradition. The Fifth Ecumenical Council endorsed the Cyrilline reading of the Chalcedonian definition for which Justinian had pressed. Henceforth that definition was read subject to the following qualifications: (1) the person (*hypostasis*) who became incarnate is identical with the second person of the Trinity, (2) Cyril's favoured expression—'one incarnate nature of God the Word'—was acceptable, if properly interpreted, (3) 'theopaschite' language about 'God suffering in the flesh' was endorsed.

As for the philosophical tradition, with Justinian's closing of the Platonic Academy at Athens in 529, public teaching of pagan philosophy was outlawed. However, the impact of this must be qualified, first, by the fact that much Platonic thought had already been absorbed into Christian theology (not least in the ascetic tradition), and secondly, by the growing popularity of the works ascribed to Dionysius the Areopagite from the 6th century onwards. This body of writings, the *Corpus Dionysiacum*, although ascribed to the apostle Paul's Athenian convert, was probably composed in the early years of the 6th century. It gave expression to a powerful cosmic vision, drawing on much earlier Christian theology (notably that associated with the Cappadocian Fathers and John Chrysostom), but clothed this in the terminology and concepts of the late Athenian Neoplatonism of such as Proclus (d. 485) and Damascius (the last head of the Platonic Academy). Through the influence of Dionysius, and through the interest of lay intellectuals in pagan philosophy which surfaced from time to time, Neoplatonism continued to influence Byzantine theology.

The 7th and 8th centuries saw a further refining of the dogmatic tradition, but, even more significantly, the creation of an enduring synthesis of these traditions in the thought of Maximos the Confessor and the epitomizing genius of John of Damascus. The refining of the dogmatic tradition occurred as a result of principled rejection of both the final attempt to heal the rifts caused by Chalcedon, and the imperial prohibition of religious imagery. In the 7th century, the Byzantine emperor was seeking to heal the politically weakening divisions in the church exposed by the Persian invasion of the eastern provinces in the 610s and 620s; he hoped, by means of this policy, to win back the provinces lost to the Arabs in the 630s and 640s. Concurrently, the final refinement of Orthodox christology was being fashioned, principally by Maximos, called 'Confessor' as his stubborn resistance to the imperial will led to suffering and exile that cost him his life. The imperial compromise—monenergism and later monothelitism—built on the Cyrilline Chalcedonianism of the 6th century, and tried to achieve union with the Monophysites on the basis of the confession of one activity (or energy), or one will, in Christ: a single composite activity or will—divine-human, 'theandric'. Maximos, no less committed to Cyrilline Chalcedonianism, saw in this compromise a complete betrayal of the theology of the Incarnation, for if God the creator did not respect the integrity of creation in his saving of humankind, then Christian theology, with its conviction of a God who creates out of love, is bankrupt. This conviction of the integrity of God's creation, even after the Fall (the effects of which he does not underestimate), lies at the heart of Maximos' synthesis of the several strands of Byzantine theology. For Maximos the cosmos and humankind reflect each other: the human being is a little cosmos, in whom all the divisions of the cosmos meet, while the cosmos is like a great human being, manifesting God's glory and, through humanity, created in the image of God, drawn back into the unity of God. The fall of humankind has shattered this harmony, which can only be restored by the Son of God's taking on himself human nature and thus fulfilling the work of reconciliation that is the intended role of humankind, as 'bond of the cosmos'. The work of the Incarnation is accomplished in the cosmos through the attempts of each human being, through faith in the Incarnate One, to achieve unity in its own 'little cosmos' by ascetic struggle, and also by the grace of the sacraments, especially the Eucharist. The cosmic dimension of the Eucharist is expressed in the structure of the church building, which reflected the idea of the church as an image of the cosmos. In Maximos' theology, these ascetic, liturgical, and dogmatic strands are woven together in a vision of the cosmos, expressed in the philosophical language of Neoplatonism, drawn from Dionysius.

It was not in Byzantium proper, Constantinople, that Maximos' theological synthesis first came to be assimilated, for there the traditions of the imperial theological compromise that Maximos opposed still held sway. Rather it was in Palestine, where Christians now found themselves politically powerless under the Muslim Umayyads, that the Maximian synthesis became the basis of the theology of those who accepted the tradition of the Byzantine Ecumenical Councils, including the Sixth (Constantinople III, 681) which had endorsed Maximos' christology. Deprived of imperial support, Byzantine Christians in Palestine had to defend their position against Monophysites, Monothelites, and other Christian heretics (who reviled them as 'Maximians'), as well as Jews and Muslims. This process, belonging to the 7th and 8th centuries, reached its culmination in the theology of John of Damascus, one-time Umayyad civil servant, who spent the last decades of his life (he died *c.*750) in one of the Palestinian monasteries, by tradition the Great Lavra, the monastery of Mar Saba. His greatest work, the *Fount of Knowledge*, is an epitome of the Maximian theological synthesis. The first two parts—the *Philosophical Chapters* and *On Heresies*—provide the logic and clearly defined terminology needed to state and defend Orthodoxy, and an account of one hundred typical misinterpretations. The final part, *On the Orthodox Faith*, expounds that faith in a hundred chapters, mostly drawn from the writings of revered fathers of the church. This exposition of the faith covers not only doctrinal matters, but also matters of cosmology and the structure of human nature, both physiological and psychological (which John regarded as profoundly interlinked). This short work was to be translated into most Christian languages, including Church Slavonic and Latin, the former nourishing the Slavs who, from the 9th century onwards, embraced Byzantine Christianity, the latter providing both a convenient summary of the patristic dogmatic tradition for the scholastics, and a pattern for their *Summas*. In John's own time this theological synthesis received its first testing in the iconoclast controversy, for clearest amongst the voices opposing the imperial decree was that of the monk John.

As well as being concerned with the place of religious imagery, the iconoclast controversy led to clarification of other theological matters, not least in the matter of eucharistic doctrine, where the iconoclast idea of the Eucharist as itself a symbol led the Orthodox to insist that the presence of Christ in the Eucharist is not symbolic but involves a real ontological change. In other ways, too, the iconoclast controversy marked a watershed in Byzantine theology and religious life. On the one hand, the ending of iconoclasm coincided with a renewal of the monastic life, heralded by the Studite reform of Theodore in the interlude between the first and second periods of iconoclasm. Its final ending was marked by the issuing of the *Synodikon of Orthodoxy*, a piece of performance art, consisting of acclamations and anathemas, read henceforth on the first Sunday of Lent, the 'Sunday of Orthodoxy'. All this had the effect of underlining the Orthodoxy of the Byzantine Church.

The renewal of monasticism led to a deepening sense of the importance of the inner wisdom represented by the monks. A pivotal figure in this, controversial in his time, was Symeon the New Theologian (949–1022). His theology, expressed in monastic catecheses, centuries of 'chapters', and poems, lays stress on the experience of God as the heart of theology. Theology is, as the monastic tradition had long maintained, experience of God, healing and transfiguring human nature. This led Symeon to stress that feature of the monastic tradition that tended to subordinate the priestly hierarchy to the experiential authority of the ascetic. Going back to the 3rd-century Alexandrian theologians, Clement and Origen, this tradition is found both in Dionysius and in monastic tales such as those in John Moschus' *Spiritual Meadow*, where we read of priest-monks who celebrated the Eucharist only after receiving a divine vision during the preparation. For Symeon this principle applied to spiritual direction, including the sacrament of penance, which was the preserve of the holy ascetic rather than the priest. The authority of (monastic) holiness was fostered by the monastic foundations contemporary with Symeon, especially those on the holy mountain of Athos (where the Great Lavra was founded by Athanasios the Athonite in 963).

The *Synodikon of Orthodoxy* received only minor modifications in the 9th and 10th centuries, but from the accession of Alexios Komnenos in 1081 it was used to bolster the fragile authority of the Komnene emperors by presenting the emperor as the guardian of Orthodoxy. With the flourishing humanism of the 11th century, there had been renewed interest in pagan philosophy and Neoplatonism (including magic and astrology), especially in the circle of the learned layman (and occasional monk), Michael Psellos. For mainly political reasons, Michael's pupil and successor as 'consul of the philosophers', John Italos, was condemned at a trial in 1082, an event commemorated by a new section of the *Synodikon*, embodying a comprehensive condemnation of the 'exterior wisdom'. Alexios' grandson, Manuel, continued this process with theological debates, held under his aegis, about questions connected with the theological issue that was to dominate politics as long as the Byzantine empire survived: that of relations with the west. The two debates, the conclusions of which were appended to the *Synodikon*, were on the question of whether the eucharistic sacrifice was offered to God the Father, or to the Trinity, and whether the interpretation of Christ's saying 'The Father is greater than I' is Trinitarian or christological. Both concerned issues raised by theologians in the west as part of the renewal of theological activity associated with the 12th-century renaissance. After the fall of Constantinople to the crusaders in 1204, the problem of relations with the west became even more urgent. Byzantine emperors accepted humiliating terms at union councils at Lyons (1274) and Florence (1438–45), but these had little impact on the Byzantine Church, nor did these concessions find their way into the *Synodikon*. Perhaps the most important theological issue dividing east and west was the *filioque* controversy: does the Holy Spirit proceed from the Father (as the creed endorsed by the Second Ecumenical Council affirmed) or from the Father and the Son (as the Latin version of the creed came to affirm by the addition of the term *filioque*)? This was first raised against Latin theologians in 7th-century Constantinople, and made a public issue by the patriarch of Constantinople, Photius, in the 9th, though many Byzantine theologians regarded the dispute as evidence of a lack of subtlety in western theology due to the deficiencies of the Latin language rather than anything more serious, at least until the 13th century.

The 'official' line of Byzantine theology, represented by the *Synodikon of Orthodoxy*, and the monastic tradition converge in the last major theological controversy of the Byzantine empire. This concerned hesychasm, a monastic movement that traced its tradition back through Symeon the New Theologian and laid emphasis on the transforming nature of prayer. The word 'hesychasm' derives from the Greek word for quietness, *hesychia*: hesychasts devoted themselves to solitary quietness in which they prayed for the acquisition of the Holy Spirit, and maintained that the goal of such prayer was a transforming vision of God, in which they beheld the uncreated light of the Godhead, and were deified. Although the hesychasts came to represent a theological position opposed to the scholasticism of the contemporary west, the origins of the dispute lay entirely within the tensions of Byzantine theology, and in particular involved the interpretation of Dionysius the Areopagite. Those opposed to the hesychasts interpreted the negative, apophatic theology of Dionysius in intellectual terms: the utterly transcendent God is known through negations, in the sense that he is beyond knowledge altogether, including the experiential knowledge claimed by the hesychasts. The hesychasts themselves maintained that apophatic theology was a theology, or experience of God in prayer, that, by denying the adequacy of all that we affirm about God, reaches beyond any knowledge about him to an encounter (or union) with God himself; and they accused their opponents of interpreting Dionysius in terms of the exterior wisdom or pagan philosophy. A further factor in the dispute was the use of techniques of prayer— use of the Jesus prayer ('Lord Jesus Christ, Son of God, have mercy on me, a sinner'), its recitation synchronized with one's breathing, and even a crouched posture—which were ridiculed by the opponents of hesychasm, especially Barlaam, a Greek monk from Calabria. The greatest defender of the hesychasts was Gregory Palamas (c.1296–1359), who had himself been a monk on Mount Athos, and eventually became archbishop of nearby Thessalonica. At the centre of his defence of hesychasm was the distinction he drew between the essence and the energies of God: the essence is unknowable, but the energies are knowable, yet both essence and energies are equally God, and uncreated. He defended the experience claimed by the hesychasts of being transfigured in the uncreated light of the Godhead, the very same light that radiated from Christ on the Mount of the Transfiguration, and even the use of physical techniques (though he laid little stress on these, regarding them as sometimes useful for beginners). Gregory was supported by the monks of Athos, but not, to begin with, by the authorities in Constantinople. However, with the accession of John Kantouzenos to the imperial throne in 1347, Gregory was vindicated at synods in the capital, and canonized in 1368 within a decade of his death. The principles of his defence of hesychasm are enshrined in the final addition to the *Synodikon of Orthodoxy*. Hesychasm was, however, a movement embracing more than monastic practice: one of Gregory's supporters, a layman called Nicolas Kavasilas, expounded his understanding of the Christian life both in a commentary on the divine liturgy, and also in his *Life in Christ*, which roots that life in the sacraments. Hesychasm, or Palamism, represents the deepest assimilation of the monastic and dogmatic traditions, combined with a repudiation of the philosophical notions of the exterior wisdom. Although Palamism had little immediate impact on Orthodox theology after the fall of Constantinople in 1453, Orthodox theological reflection being then too bound up with defining itself in largely western terms in relation to Catholicism and Protestantism, the hesychast revival associated with the *Philokalia* of Nikodimos the Hagiorite and Makarios of Corinth (published 1782), its reception by Slav Orthodoxy, and its importance for the Paris school of Orthodox theology in the 20th century have led to hesychasm's becoming definitive for modern Orthodox theology as never before.

As well as the controversy over hesychasm, the final decades of the Byzantine empire saw an unparalleled renewal of Byzantine humanism: interest in Plato, Aristotle, and the Neoplatonists revived, as well as in contemporary movements in western theology and philosophy (Aquinas's *Summa contra Gentiles* was translated into Greek in 1354). This had little lasting effect on Byzantine theology, and indeed had less impact on the emerging Italian Renaissance than is often claimed. It was the monks with their interior wisdom, not the scholars with their exterior wisdom, who survived the final collapse of the Byzantine empire to the Turks, and it was among the monks that traditions of Byzantine theology were preserved most faithfully, and among them that the seeds of renewal took root and eventually bore fruit.

Krivochéine, B., *Dans la lumière du Christ: S. Syméon le Nouveau Théologien 949–1022: Vie—Spiritualité—Doctrine* (1980).

Lossky, V., *The Mystical Theology of the Eastern Church* (1957).

Louth, A., *Maximus the Confessor* (1996).

Meyendorff, J., *St Gregory Palamas* (1964).

—— *Byzantine Theology* (1974).

—— *The Byzantine Legacy in the Orthodox Church* (1982).

Pelikan, J., *The Spirit of Eastern Christendom (600–1700)* (1974).

Runciman, S., *The Last Byzantine Renaissance* (1970).

V

HOPE AND TRANSFORMATION
Eastern Orthodox theology

Kallistos Ware

T HE ORTHODOX CHURCH, LARGELY ISOLATED FROM
the west until the 20th century, has begun during
the last hundred years to exercise a limited yet significant influence upon western thinking. Following the
fall of the Byzantine empire (1453), Orthodox Christianity in
the Greek lands and the rest of the Balkans entered its 'dark
ages', the period of Ottoman domination, extending until the
19th century; this allowed little opportunity to eastern Christians
for creative development of theology. In Russia, however, outside
Turkish rule, there emerged from the 1840s onwards an independent and at times strikingly original approach to religious questions. It was in 19th-century Russia that the first serious encounter
occurred between Orthodoxy and Enlightenment and post-
Enlightenment thought.

Russian religious thought in the 20th century continued to
display exceptional vitality, first in Russia itself until the 1917 Revolution, thereafter in the western world. The main intellectual
centres of Russian *émigré* theology have been the Institute of St
Sergius in Paris, which enjoyed an era of great brilliance between
the two World Wars, and more recently St Vladimir's Seminary in
New York. From the 1960s onwards theologians of international
stature appeared also in Greece and Romania. Orthodox debates
in the 19th and 20th centuries concentrated upon three major
topics: the nature of theology, the doctrine of creation, and the

essence of the church. Relatively little attention has been given to biblical studies.

How should we theologize? Byzantine thought, especially towards the end of the empire, tended to be highly conservative. 'The great men of the past', observed Theodore Metochites (1270–1332), 'have expressed everything so perfectly that they have left nothing more for us to say.' Yet especially in the realm of mystical theology Byzantium continued to produce original thinkers of the first rank such as Symeon the New Theologian (959–1022) and Gregory Palamas (1296–1359). The Turkish period, however, was marked by an inflexible theological traditionalism. As Patriarch Jeremias II of Constantinople stated in 1590, 'It is not the practice of our church to innovate in any way whatsoever, whereas the western church innovates unceasingly.'

Nevertheless this conservatism was counterbalanced by a strongly westernizing trend within Orthodox thought during the 17th and 18th centuries. The absence of Christian universities in the Ottoman world meant that most Orthodox theologians obtained their training in the west, under Roman Catholic or Protestant teachers, and inevitably this led them to adopt western terminology and styles of argument, resulting in what the Russian theologian Georges Florovsky has termed a 'pseudomorphosis'.

It was the Russian Slavophiles in the mid-19th century who first strove to break free from this 'Babylonian captivity' (Florovsky's phrase). Ivan Kireevsky (1806–56) rebelled against what he saw as the rationalism of the west, its excessive reliance upon discursive argumentation. 'Rome', he affirmed in somewhat sweeping terms, 'preferred the abstract syllogism to sacred tradition, which is the expression of the common mind of the whole Christian world, and in which that world coheres as a living and indissoluble unity' (Collected Works (1911), i. 226). Truth for the Slavophiles was not to be attained by the isolated individual relying solely on the reasoning brain's logic, but could be discovered only within the organic life of the church, through shared experience and interpersonal communion. 'The knowledge of the truth is given to mutual love,' said Aleksei Khomyakov (1804–60).

Fundamental to all religious understanding, according to Khomyakov, is the spirit of *sobornost* (literally 'catholicity'), by which he meant unanimity in freedom, the grace-given possibility whereby the church's members, without sacrificing personal liberty, are enabled to attain a common mind. The Slavophiles took as their model the corporate consciousness to be found (so they believed) in the Russian peasant commune; in Turgenev's phrase (originally applied to Herzen), they 'sought salvation in a sheep-skin coat'. But their sources were not exclusively Russian: they were influenced also by German Idealist philosophy, especially by Hegel and Schelling.

Leading Russian theologians in the 20th-century emigration, Florovsky and Vladimir Lossky (1903–58) for example, agreed with Kireevsky and Khomyakov in repudiating undue dependence upon the west, but they reacted sharply against the Slavophile attempt to identify a specifically Russian approach to theology. They advocated instead a return to the Greek fathers. Florovsky, a firm upholder of 'Christian Hellenism', summed up his theological programme in the phrase 'neo-patristic synthesis'. He meant, not simply mechanical repetition of the words of the fathers, but rather a creative recovery of the 'patristic mind'. The fathers are to be treated not as voices from the distant past but as contemporary witnesses; they are to be not only quoted but questioned, for holy tradition represents the critical spirit of the church.

For Florovsky and Lossky, as for a later generation of *émigré* Russian theologians including Alexander Schmemann (1921–83) and John Meyendorff (1926–92), the notion of the 'patristic mind' signified above all the integral link between theology and prayer. In the much-quoted words of the 4th-century desert father Evagrius of Pontus, 'If you are a theologian, you will pray truly; and if you pray truly, you are a theologian' (*On Prayer*, 60). All authentic theology is therefore liturgical and mystical. 'Far from being mutually opposed,' stated Lossky, 'theology and mysticism support and complete each other. One is impossible without the other.'

A similar approach is evident in contemporary Greek writers such as John Romanides (b. 1927) and Christos Yannaras (b. 1935). Yannaras, influenced by Heidegger as well as Lossky, rejects the 'academic scientism' which in his view dominates the work of older Greek theologians. Theology is 'not an intellectual discipline but an experiential communion, a participation'. It is 'a fruit of the interior purity of the Christian's spiritual life', to be 'identified with the vision of God . . . with the personal experience of the transfiguration of creation by uncreated grace'.

Yannaras's reference to cosmic transfiguration brings us to a second dominant theme in modern Orthodox theology: the doctrine of creation. Here two main tendencies are apparent. There is first the school of Sophiology, represented by three Russian thinkers, Vladimir Soloviev (1853–1900), Pavel Florensky (1882–1937), and the former Marxist Sergii Bulgakov (1871–1944), who understand the relationship between God and the world in terms of Sophia or Holy Wisdom. In Bulgakov's thought, which is complex and frequently obscure, Sophia is both divine and creaturely. Divine Sophia (not a person or *hypostasis*) signifies God's eternal plan of creation, and more particularly the uncreated freedom which enables the divine life to empty itself in the act of creation and to mirror itself in that which is not God. Self-emptying or kenosis, a pivotal concept for Bulgakov, is to be seen not only in the Incarnation of the Son but also in God's decision to create the world and even in the eternal life of the Trinity. On the creaturely side, Sophia denotes creation's response to God, the impulse within all created things towards harmony and order, their longing or *eros* for divine Beauty. Uncreated and created Sophia are united supremely in the person of Christ.

Turning to the second tendency, we find the sophiological approach vehemently repudiated by the 'neo-patristic' group. Bulgakov was attacked above all by Lossky, who maintained that he had confused the levels of person (*hypostasis*) and nature (*physis*). Kenosis, Lossky argued, involves the Second Person of the Trinity, the incarnate Logos, but it cannot be equated with the divine nature. To interpret the relationship between God and the world, the neo-patristic group preferred the cosmological teachings of Maximus the Confessor (c.580–662) and Gregory Palamas.

The Romanian theologian Dumitru Staniloae (1903–93) has drawn especially upon Maximus' notion of the immanent *logoi*. Within each created thing the creator Logos has implanted a *logos* or inner principle which makes that thing uniquely itself, and which at the same time draws it to union with God. Thus the world is a theophany, a sacrament of God's presence; all created things are God's 'garments', and each is a divine 'word' spoken to us personally. The human being, as high priest of the creation, has the vocation of rendering these *logoi* manifest, and so of transfiguring the cosmos. 'Man puts the seal of his understanding and of his intelligent work on to creation, thereby humanizing it and giving it, humanized, back to God. He actualizes the world's potentialities. Thus the world is not only a gift but a task for man' (*Sobornost*, 5. 9 (1969), 665).

In his understanding of the creation, Staniloae also employs, as do Florovsky, Lossky, Meyendorff, Romanides, and Yannaras, the essence–energies distinction developed by Palamas. The divine essence denotes God's transcendence, the energies his immanence. God's essence remains for ever radically unknowable to all created beings, not only in the present age but in the age to come. The energies, on the other hand—which are not an intermediary or a created gift but God himself in his direct, unmediated action—permeate the universe, filling all things with uncreated grace and glory.

By using this distinction between divine essence and divine energies, the neo-Palamites seek to affirm without compromise both God's otherness and his nearness. The apophatic mystery of God is safeguarded, but the creator is also seen as everywhere present: not pantheism, but pan*en*theism. Some western theologians, both Roman Catholic and Anglican, consider that the essence–energies distinction impairs God's simplicity and indivisibility, but others have incorporated it in their own thinking. Manifestly the theological categories of Palamism differ from those of Thomism; each system deserves to be judged by its own criteria.

Closely linked with Palamite theology, although not identical, is the hesychast tradition of mystical prayer (*hesychia* meaning inner silence, stillness of heart). The classical expression of hesychasm is the *Philokalia*, a vast collection of spiritual texts edited by Macarius of Corinth (1731–1805) and Nicodemus of the Holy Mountain (1748–1809). First published in 1782, it has enjoyed a growing popularity among both Orthodox and non-Orthodox Christians during the last fifty years. In the eyes of many, this hesychast renaissance, with its devotion to the Jesus Prayer, represents the most dynamic element in contemporary Orthodox spirituality.

We turn now to the third theme, the church. For the Slavophiles the decisive factor in ecclesial life is not power of jurisdiction but mutual love. In the words of Khomyakov's disciple George Samarin (1819–79), 'The church is not a doctrine, nor a system, nor an institution. She is a living organism, the organism of truth and love, or rather she is truth and love as an organism.' The corporate consciousness or *sobornost* of the church is manifested above all in councils. A church council, while attended primarily by the hierarchy, acquires ecumenical authority only if 'received' by the whole body of the church, including the laity.

Orthodox theologians in the 20th century have criticized Slavophile ecclesiology for its lack of precision, its diminution of the teaching *charisma* of the episcopate, and its failure to emphasize the sacramental character of the church. Khomyakov's notion of *sobornost*, based as it is upon the sociological model of the Russian peasant commune, reduces supranatural church communion to a naturalistic level. Following Ignatius of Antioch (d. *c*.107), the Russian Nicolas Afanassieff (1893–1966) and the Greek John Zizioulas, Metropolitan of Pergamon (b. 1931), prefer to envisage the church not in sociological but in eucharistic terms. In full agreement with the Roman Catholic writer Henri de Lubac, they maintain that it is the Eucharist that makes the church; participation in holy communion actualizes the church as the body of Christ and maintains it in unity. The Eucharist can take place only locally, and so the local church possesses crucial significance. The title 'catholic' applies not primarily to the church as a world-wide association, but to each local assembly at which the Eucharist is celebrated.

Zizioulas has employed the concept of communion not only in his ecclesiology but also in his understanding of the human person. Our humanness is realized through interpersonal relationship; there is no true person unless there are at least two persons in communication with each other. Created in the image of the triune God, we become genuinely human only through reciprocal love after the model of Trinitarian perichoresis. Such is also the viewpoint of Staniloae, who writes: 'The Trinity alone assures our existence as persons.'

It is a striking fact that, since the First World War, the growing-points of Orthodox theology have been not so much in the traditional Orthodox lands as in the west, in Paris and New York, for example. Orthodoxy can no longer be regarded as exclusively 'eastern'. The fall of communism opened up fresh and exciting possibilities in Russia and eastern Europe, and perhaps the centre of intellectual influence will now shift back eastwards; but the pattern of the future remains uncertain. For Russian Orthodoxy, as for the Orthodox world in general, this is an unsettled era, a time of danger but also of great hope.

Blane, A., Raeff, M., and Williams, G. H., *Georges Florovsky: Russian Intellectual and Orthodox Churchman* (1993).

Bulgakov, Sergii, *Towards a Russian Political Theology*, ed. Rowan Williams (1999).

Lossky, V., *The Mystical Theology of the Eastern Church* (1957).

McPartlan, P., *The Eucharist Makes the Church: Henri de Lubac and John Zizioulas in Dialogue* (1993).

Nichols, A., *Light from the East: Authors and Themes in Orthodox Theology* (1995).

Pain, J., and Zernov, N., *A Bulgakov Anthology* (1976).

Sopko, A. J., *Prophet of Roman Orthodoxy: The Theology of John Romanides* (1998).

Staniloae, D., *The Experience of God* (1994).

Williams, R., 'Eastern Orthodox Theology', in D. F. Ford (ed.), *The Modern Theologians*, 2nd edn. (1997).

Yannaras, C., 'Theology in Present-Day Greece', *St. Vladimir's Seminary Quarterly*, 16/4 (1972).

Zernov, N., *The Russian Religious Renaissance of the Twentieth Century* (1963).

Zizioulas, J. D., *Being as Communion: Studies in Personhood and the Church* (1985).

VI

IDENTITY AND CONTINUITY
The Armenian tradition

Vigen Guroian

IN 2001 THE ARMENIAN CHURCH COMMEMORATED THE 1700th year of the establishment of Christianity as the official religion of the nation. St Gregory the Illuminator (*c.* 240–332), called the Apostle of Armenia, is credited with having converted King Tiridates III and his court in the early 4th century. Most scholars now place that event in 314, just one year after Constantine's promulgation of the Edict of Milan, but 301 remains the date of tradition. Whether 301 or 314, the ancient lineage of this church of the Christian east cannot be gainsaid. And it is this lineage that has given cause for the view that Armenia was the first nation to adopt Christianity as the state religion.

Legend and tradition have it that the apostles Thaddeus and Bartholomew evangelized Armenia in the 1st century. More reliable historical evidence does show that Christian bishops were present in Armenia certainly by the middle of the 3rd century, a result of the missionary outreach of two of the great centres of the early church, Greek Caesarea and Syrian Edessa. The Armenian Church's spirituality has ever since reflected this combination of influences. Thus, early Armenian Christianity breathed in the great Trinitarian theology of the Cappadocian fathers as well as the asceticism and spirituality of Aphrahat of Persia and Ephrem the Syrian. Armenian biblical exegesis followed the methods of the Alexandrine school.

Over its first century of existence, the Armenian Church maintained ecclesiastical ties with the church in Caesarea where St Gregory himself had been educated. In 387, however, Armenia was partitioned between Rome and Persia, and the latter exerted strong pressure on the Armenians to dissolve their ties with the Greek-speaking west. The autonomy of the Armenian Church was well under way when the christological controversy over the fourth Ecumenical Council of Chalcedon (451) broke out. In 452 Hovsep I was elevated to catholicos (or patriarch), and the end of supervision by the church in Caesarea was formalized. The Armenian Church began its long journey of independence (sometimes in isolation) that over seventeen hundred years has evolved a very distinctive Christian tradition.

The breach that came to separate the churches who adhered to the Council of Chalcedon and those who did not (Syrians, Egyptian Copts, and Armenians) did not entirely cut off the Armenian Church from the mainstream of Christian theology. At the turn of the 5th century, St Mesrob and St Sahak the Great (catholicos c.389–c.438) invented an alphabet and translated the holy scriptures, first from the Syriac and then from the Greek Septuagint text. The Holy Translators and their students also supervised translations of important patristic commentaries and theological works.

Still, there is no question that the Council of Chalcedon marked an important turning-point in Armenian Christianity. The Armenians, who were not in fact present at Chalcedon, were immediately suspicious of Pope Leo's Tome and its influence upon the Council, ultimately seeing in both a taint of the Nestorian heresy. It was nearly fifty years, however, before a conciliar act was promulgated against Dyophysitism under Catholicos Babgen (490–516) in 506. And it was not until the second and third Synods of Dvin in 554 and 607 that the Council of Chalcedon was formally condemned.

But the issue did not go away. Over the centuries, the record reveals much see-sawing back and forth, as Armenian Church leaders made conciliatory gestures towards Constantinople and then Rome depending on political circumstances. For example, even in a short space of thirty years after the third Synod of Dvin, on the heels of victory over the Persians, Catholicos Ezra and an entourage of bishops and doctors formally accepted Chalcedon at a synod called together by the Emperor Heraclius. This intercommunion lasted until the end of the century. When the Sixth Ecumenical Council (680) condemned Monothelitism, to which the Armenians heartily subscribed, the shift back to a strong Monophysite position was completed. This position can be characterized by its emphatic embrace of Cyril of Alexandria's 5th-century formula 'one nature, and that incarnate, of the divine Word', stressing the unity and concreteness of the divine Word and second Person of the Trinity who fully assumed our humanity.

In the modern era, this moderate Armenian Monophysitism has proved amenable to compromise in seeking consensus with both Eastern Orthodox and Roman Catholics. In 1990 representatives of the Armenian Church signed a historic document produced by a Joint Commission of the Eastern and Oriental Orthodox Churches that called for unity and full communion between their churches based upon mutual affirmations of the orthodoxy of their respective christological teachings. And in December of 1996 Catholicos Karekin I of All Armenians (1932-1999), and Pope John Paul II issued a joint declaration in which they agreed upon a common christological formulation acceptable to both communions.

The strong theopaschal concern of Armenian christology, represented in the church's retention of Peter the Fuller's 5th-century amendment to the Trisagion, 'who was crucified for us', may be of special interest for our time. The emphasis on the suffering of God is expressed stunningly by the 6th-century Armenian philosopher and apologist David the Invincible (Anhaght) in his short work entitled 'An Encomium on the Holy Cross of God': 'Now he who laid Himself down indeed did so through and on the Cross. And He who gave Himself on it is still on it and does not distance Himself from it. . . . Therefore the Cross is the Cross of God and He Himself, the Crucified One, God immortal, uncircumscribable and infinite.' This Armenian christology and doctrine of God has much to contribute to the modern discussion of a crucified God advanced in the 20th century by the likes of Jürgen Moltmann and Hans Urs von Balthasar.

The richness and distinctiveness of the Armenian tradition can be found in other quarters as well. Eznik of Kolb championed Armenian apologetics in the 5th century. His *Refutation of the Sects* is a mine of information on Mazdean religion and the Marcionite heresy. The Armenian mystical and poetical tradition is represented in its highest form by the 10th-century saint, Gregory of Narek (Narekatsi). His greatest work is entitled *The Book of Lamentations*, a series of prayers whose tone is strongly penitential. The *Lamentations* have deeply influenced Armenian piety and spirituality. The theologically rich hymnography of the Armenian Church (this is where Armenian theology may be at its best) reaches its heights in the beautiful and profound compositions of the 12th-century catholicos, St Nerses the Gracious (Shnorhali). The 14th century produced the Armenian scholastic, St Gregory of Datev (Tatevatsi). While he championed Armenian orthodoxy against the Latins, his theology incorporates much of their thinking (notable among these influences are writings of Albert the Great, Thomas Aquinas, and Bonaventure). He adopted the language of transubstantiation in his eucharistic theology and in his discussion of baptism there is an uncharacteristic accent on original sin at the expense of a more traditional emphasis on illumination, regeneration, and entrance into the church and the body of Christ. In any case, the distinctively Latin flavour of St Gregory of Datev's theology lends positive proof of cultural and theological transmigrations between the Christian east and west more widespread than has sometimes been assumed. His best known work is the *Book of Questions*, written in the style of disputation.

The Armenian Church's liturgical practices contain some distinct variances from their Byzantine sources. The prototype of the Divine Liturgy is the Liturgy of Basil of Caesarea but with augmentations from the Liturgy of John Chrysostom and some late Latin influences. The Armenian Church gives communion in both elements, but does not mix water with the wine, and in contrast to the Byzantines uses unleavened bread.

Since the birth of a sovereign Armenian nation in 1991, the church in Armenia has enjoyed religious freedom and special privileges under a new Law on Freedom of Conscience and Religious Organizations. But the Armenian Church lacks the resources effectively to re-evangelize the people. Still, there now is reason to hope that at home and abroad the Armenian Church will recover from the devastating consequences of both the Turkish genocide of over a million Armenians during the First World War and the repression of the Soviet era.

There are over five million Armenians throughout the world, some three million in Armenia and the balance in diasporas concentrated in the old Soviet Union, North America, the Middle East, and Europe. While the Armenian Church is a *de facto* international body, whose leaders have long been active within the ecumenical movement, both at home and abroad it tenaciously remains a self-consciously national church.

Arpee, L., *A History of Armenian Christianity from the Beginning to Our Own Time* (1946).
Guroian, V., *Ethics After Christendom* (1974).
Lang, D. V., *Armenia: Cradle of Civilization* (1970).
Mouradian, C. S., *De Staline à Gorbatchev: histoire d'une république soviétique, l'Arménie* (1990).
Nersoyan, T., *Armenian Church Historical Studies* (1996).
Ormanian, M., *The Armenian Church* (1912).
Sarkissian, K., *A Brief Introduction to Armenian Christian Literature* (1960).

CHRISTIAN THOUGHT IN THE WEST

VII

HARMONY AND TRADITION
Latin theology, 4th–10th centuries

✂ + ✂

John Cavadini

THE 4TH CENTURY WITNESSED THE FLOWERING OF early Latin theology as Christianity made its transition from a *religio illicita*, the subject of periodic persecution, to established religion, the beneficiary of legal privilege, while the old Roman polytheism became the target of punitive legislation. The 4th to the 6th centuries witnessed the sharpening of features that would come to characterize Latin theology over against its Greek counterpart. Engagement with the questions and controversies exercising the east begins to be eroded by a loss of fluency in Greek in an increasingly isolated west, and, more positively, by attention to categories and issues native to the west. Over this transition towers the figure of Augustine, whose influence dominates nearly the whole of our period, both a source of inspiration and a sign of contradiction as his legacy was interpreted and contested. We must refuse the temptation to view either western or eastern theology as inherently superior, recognizing instead their complementary genius and their underlying unity.

Hilary of Poitiers (*c*.300–*c*.367) represents a style of Latin theology well acquainted with Greek language and with the controversies of the east. Elected bishop of Poitiers; deposed for anti-Arian activity; exiled to Phrygia (356); he became deeply acquainted with Origen's works and with members of the *homoeousian* party, who described the Son as 'of like nature' with the

Father, rather than 'of the same nature' (*homoousios*). He admired these men, and even, for a time, represented them (at Seleucia in 359). His *De trinitate* (356–60) combines the legacy of Tertullian and Novatian with strong anti-Sabellian and anti-Arian theologies. It shows a sympathetic confluence of homoeousian and homoousian concerns, arguing as much by appeal to biblical passages as by dialectics. His earlier exegesis (*Commentary on Matthew*) attests the state of western exegesis before Origen was much known in the west, but his *Commentary on Psalms*, written after his exile and thoroughly indebted to Origen, served to introduce Origenian themes into western theology.

Ambrose (*c*.339–97) follows Hilary in his engagement in anti-Arian polemic and in his ability to read Greek sources, including Origen, Philo, and, now, Plotinus. Ambrose, elected bishop of Milan (373 or 374) before he was baptized, gradually persuaded the Emperor Gratian to adopt anti-Arian instruction and policy, culminating in anti-heretical sanctions and in the treatises *De fide* and *De Spiritu Sancto*, which show the influence especially of Basil and of Didymus. In addition to doctrinal treatises and moral/ ascetic works (including the *De officiis* on the priesthood, and the *De virginitate*), much of his output was exegetical, mostly OT commentary (and one on Luke). These show the influence of Origen and (though Ambrose consistently denigrated philosophy and philosophers as possessed of half-truths wholly derivative from the bible) the pervasive influence of Plotinus, a source untouched by Hilary but increasingly influential in the west. Ambrose was a prominent member of the circle of Milanese Christian Neoplatonists (including Marius Victorinus) who exerted lasting influence on Augustine.

Contemporary with Ambrose are Jerome (*c*.347–419) and Rufinus (*c*.345–410), friends who, with others, embarked upon a joint ascetical and scholarly enterprise at Aquileia. Jerome copied the works of a growing canon of Christian Latin literature: Cyprian, Hilary, Tertullian; but, when Rufinus moved east with Melania (373), visiting the Origenist monks in Egypt and eventually establishing a monastery himself on the Mount of Olives,

Jerome left for Syria, where he studied Hebrew and Greek and was ordained priest at Antioch. He returned to Rome (c.382) where Pope Damasus made him his secretary and supported his project of correcting the extant Latin translations of the gospels and the psalms. After Damasus's death, Jerome left Rome and established with Paula a monastery at Bethlehem, having visited Origen's library at Caesarea on the way. Beginning in 393, he made direct translations from the Hebrew of the psalms and other biblical books. Together with his own and Rufinus the Syrian's translations of the NT, these eventually became the Vulgate, perhaps the single most influential work of the patristic Latin west.

Jerome was progressively alienated from Rufinus, Melania, and their Origenist patron, Bishop John of Jerusalem, because his own protector and friend, Epiphanius, was vehemently anti-Origenist, though Jerome's exegetical works continued to depend (more discreetly) on Origen's. Rufinus returned to Rome in 397, beginning a career of translation which, together with translations by Jerome, saved most of what remains today of Origen. When Theophilus of Alexandria condemned Origen in 400, Jerome saw to it that Pope Anastasius would repeat this condemnation (which he did in two letters), and this effectively cut off appeal to Origen's systematic theology in the west (though his exegesis was read in all centuries). Thus the 4th century ends with the eclipse of Origen's delicate synthesis of Middle Platonism and Christian faith, with its tracing of the origin of evil and balancing of 'nature' and 'grace' (as they would later be called in the west). As knowledge of Greek ebbed, the sophisticated syntheses of Origen's eastern heirs, the Cappadocians, became equally unavailable for sustained theological use.

Augustine of Hippo was to have the problem of forging a new synthesis of Christian faith and reason without much benefit from earlier solutions. He began his theological career in an anti-Manichaean mode, following the lead of Ambrose in using the philosophical monism of Neoplatonism to combat Manichaean dualism. Augustine's insistence that all being, *qua* being, is good, and that evil is not being but rather the corruption of being, unites him with all Platonist theologians of antiquity. Increasingly, however, tensions inherent in the Neoplatonic anthropology, tensions that Ambrose tended to overlook and that traditionalist Origenist theologians such as Jerome solved in other ways, began to bother Augustine. In his earliest works, he repeats Porphyry's injunction that 'Everything bodily must be avoided,' and interprets the creation of the sexes in Genesis 2 allegorically. But once ordained (392) and working as a pastor, he began to acquire greater familiarity with and sympathy for scripture, so that these strategies, anti-Manichaean in intent, came to seem Manichaean themselves. Augustine's study of St Paul just after his consecration as bishop of Hippo (395) refined his sense of sin as interior conflict within the soul, rather than conflict between soul and body. His theology begins to emphasize the positive character of bodily nature as originally created, and (in reaction against Jerome's radically ascetic views), of marriage and sex even after the Fall.

Instead of focusing on the body as the origin of sin, Augustine focused on the will, its freedom vitiated in the pride of Adam and Eve, who wished to create and hold on to a fellowship with each other independent of God, replacing, in effect, God's central place in the universe with their own. Human societies obsessively re-enact this prideful desire to find in themselves a self-sufficient good. Individuals inherit a nature vitiated by the effects of original sin and can be healed only by the special, predestined intervention of God's grace. The Incarnation of the Son, the Word and Wisdom of God, is a moving act of humility on God's part, and this spectacle of God's abject humility moves those whose hearts have been restored to health by grace; though for others the proclamation of the gospel will, even if heard, fall on deaf ears. The controversy with Pelagius (411–17) and its vigorous afterlife in the controversy with Julian of Eclanum did not substantially alter Augustine's position, though it refined his understanding of the precise operation of grace.

The change in Augustine's theology from Neoplatonic optimism based on theories of human perfectibility is often regarded as disillusionment or as a turn towards pessimism about the human condition, but it can also be viewed in opposite terms: his sense of the insidious complicity in evil which binds all humanity together and constitutes its 'original sin' makes him more sensitive to the life of the Christian believer as one of continuous healing and transformation rather than one of static perfection. Growth in the spiritual life is not restricted to a philosophic few, but is equally available to those in any walk of life, regardless of distinctions of education, class, or marital status. Augustine certainly thought virginity superior to marriage, but both were equally liable to succumb to temptation (marriage to lust and virginity to pride), and transformation and healing were available equally to both in Christ. As one comes to identify one's sufferings and trials with the sufferings of the Word made flesh, all people can find in the active life the beginning of the contemplative vision of God's Wisdom. The Neoplatonic 'ascent' from consideration of creatures to contemplation of God needs no special philosophical training; in fact it is possible only by clinging in faith to the 'wood', the cross of Christ, in which God's humble Wisdom is fully revealed. Bonaventure, Dante, and other theologians of the high medieval period would develop this theme further.

Against the Donatists, Augustine had argued that the sacraments belong to Christ, not to the minister of the sacrament, and their efficacy depends not on the moral character of the minister but on the valid celebration of the sacrament and its reception in faith. In receiving baptism (for example), one places one's faith in Christ, not in the minister (whose character is, in any event, hidden from us). Such an 'objective theory' of the operation of the sacraments may seem in tension with Augustine's theory of grace imparted internally and specially, but they are actually complementary. Anti-Donatist and anti-Pelagian arguments both pictured a church composed not of the perfected but of those being healed from imperfection, the 'inn' which the Good Samaritan Jesus had founded for our cure. The Eucharist in particular, as the universally celebrated sacrifice of Christ, is the locus of continuing re-formation. Both the anti-Donatist and the anti-Pelagian polemic emphasize the 'mixed' character of human life, in the church (where those predestined to life and those not so predestined exist together); in the individual (where faith prompted by grace is always operative in the midst of competing desires and motivations); and in society at large (where even the best of cultural activity, e.g. the liberal arts, is not free from the corruption of pride and cannot lead anyone to God apart from the preaching of the gospel, the sacraments, and the inner working of grace). Augustine's theology thus affirms that the best in social and cultural reality can be transformed in the hands of those converted by grace, but he retains a critical distance from any particular cultural system. This is a direct result of his theology of grace which was to distinguish theology in the west from eastern theologies more inclined to identify themselves with particular cultures. In the conviction that all human nature, no matter how vitiated by sin, could be transformed by grace (even if not all would be) as in the deepening of the sense of hope for transformation available to all, one sees the completion of Augustine's original anti-Manichaean polemic, contrary to charges both ancient and modern that he returned to Manichaean dualism in his rather physical analysis of the transmission of original sin. The sense that the wonder of grace restores the wonder of nature echoes resoundingly in later theology from Hildegard to Bonaventure to Pascal.

Augustine recognized a canon of western Christian authors (Hilary, Ambrose, and those mentioned in *De doctrina*, 4) though he rarely felt the need to appeal to any of them as authorities unless his opponents had. He anticipated his own inclusion in the canon, cataloguing a library of his own writings. They were immediately anthologized, beginning with Prosper of Aquitaine, whose *Sententiae* excerpted passages for use against John Cassian (*c*.360–435), Faustus of Riez (*c*.400–*c*.490), and other semi-Pelagians. These agreed with Augustine on the universal necessity for baptism and for direct interior infusion of grace, but disagreed on the extent of the damage done by original sin, admitting some remaining natural capacity for initiating (but not completing) salvation in advance of grace. The 5th-century dispute over the Augustinian theology of grace was resolved at the Council of Orange (529), which upheld Augustinian teaching on the necessity and prevenience of grace, condemning semi-Pelagian teachings without explicitly condemning the semi-Pelagians as heretics, and disowning double predestination (predestination to damnation as well as to salvation), always a pitfall in Augustinian doctrine.

Cassian had lived in the Egyptian desert, and Faustus had been both monk and abbot at Lérins, established by Honoratus on principles observed on his own journeys east, so both had roots in eastern monastic spirituality. This was based on eastern views of the Fall as less serious: an evil but immature mistake of childlike beings who even before sin needed to be educated to a higher, freer state. The Rule of St Benedict (c.530) may be regarded as a resolution, on the spiritual level, of the 5th-century debates on grace; perhaps the most enduring resolution of all, one of the few places where east and west met so fruitfully. It embraces the developmental view of Cassian and Basil, but in the conviction that the central act of asceticism is the formation of a community of mutual love and service and that only grace can call such a community into being out of the 'nothing' of an assortment of individuals of varying temperament and unequal social rank, we recognize the legacy of Augustine.

Augustine was influential in other 5th- and 6th-century debates and movements. Vincent of Lérins' *Excerpta* anthologized passages for use against Nestorianism, and Eugippius's *Excerpta* collected passages on a variety of topics. In North Africa Fulgentius of Ruspe excerpted and glossed Augustine's trinitarian works in controversy with the Vandal Arians. Augustine's *De doctrina*, with its insistence on the utility of secular learning for Christian exegetes and its catalogue of great Christian stylists, inspired Cassiodorus, whose *Institutes* chartered a vision of education to which all the great educators and encyclopedists of the 7th–9th centuries were heirs: Bede in Britain, Isidore in Spain, Rabanus Maurus in Germany, Alcuin in Gaul, Remigius of

Auxerre, and Odo, founder of Cluny. These and other early medieval writers were heavily dependent not only on Augustine, but on Jerome and Gregory the Great (c.540–604) as well. Gregory's exegesis (*Moralia in Job*; 40 Gospel Homilies; homilies on Ezekiel and the Song of Songs) and pastoral theology (in the Letters and *Pastoral Rule*) were especially influential and were themselves anthologized.

The early medieval centuries are often underestimated by historians who scorn the theology and exegesis of the period as wholly derivative. But to see the true creativity of the period, one must look at the *use* of sources. The scriptural commentaries of Bede, Alcuin, Rabanus, and others may cite long passages from the church fathers word for word, but selecting and editing citations is a process of interpretation: it both establishes the fathers as authoritative tradition and seeks to clarify their meaning, especially in view of contemporary questions. For example, Alcuin's huge *Commentary* on John is drawn mainly from Augustine's, yet Alcuin's skilful work of redaction gives his edition an entirely new cast, concerned less with the self-disclosure and hiddenness of God, and more with the question of how Christ is both divine and human, reflecting Alcuin's role in the Adoptionism controversy. This controversy, which began in Spain in the 8th century as an argument between Elipandus of Toledo and Beatus of Liebana, spilled over into Carolingian realms when Alcuin attacked Felix of Urgel, accusing him of Nestorianism, that is of teaching that Jesus was adopted as God's Son and so exists as a second person beside the eternal person of the Word. One could regard this dispute partly as concerned with interpreting western christological sources such as Leo I and (especially) Augustine. Similarly, the hostile western reception of the decisions of Nicaea II (787), resolving the eastern iconoclast controversies in favour of the veneration of icons, was due partly to a bad translation of the decrees and partly to increasing tension between east and west over issues such as the insertion of the *filioque* into the creed. But it was also due to a conviction culled from western sources that icon-worship (which the bad translation made Nicaea II seem to be approving) was wrong. The *Libri Carolini* (late 780s) drew heavily upon previous western sources, especially Augustine's *De doctrina* and Gregory the Great's letter to Serenus.

Ninth-century controversies between the monk Gottschalk and Hincmar of Rheims over predestination represented another attempt to interpret the patristic inheritance. Gottschalk, arguing an exaggerated Augustinian position, was condemned and imprisoned. Hincmar relied partly on Hilary of Poitiers' *Commentary on the Psalms* to rebut Gottschalk, and thus, perhaps without knowing it, mitigated extreme Augustinianism by appeal to Origen, whose work inspired Hilary's *Commentary* and who could now affect the controversy under the unimpeachably authoritative name of Hilary. A similar creative appeal to authorities characterizes Hincmar's *De una et non trina deitate*, defending, against Gottschalk and Ratramnus, his replacement of the hymn phrase 'trina deitas' as promoting tritheism. Another controversy, between Paschasius Radbertus and Ratramnus, both monks of Corbie, on the Eucharist, is often thought to foreshadow Reformation debates, with Radbertus upholding a more 'realist' view and Ratramnus a more 'symbolic' one. In fact, both defend what we would call the Real Presence, but the language chosen to describe this, and the precise bodily presence in question, were the issues under debate as both sides, especially Ratramnus, claimed Augustine as warrant.

The most daring and creative intellect in the whole period between the collapse of the western empire and the year 1000 is John Scotus Eriugena (*c.*810–77), whose *Periphyseon* was an attempt to synthesize eastern and western sources into a unified theology. This was preceded by his translation into Latin of what would come to be, after Augustine, the single most influential theological source in high medieval theology, the works of Pseudo-Dionysius (5th–6th centuries). The *Periphyseon* uses Greek sources (Dionysius, Gregory Nazianzen, Gregory of Nyssa, Maximus, etc.), attempting to integrate Augustine into their outlook. The results are not as forced as one might think. Eriugena is skilful in finding and emphasizing points of contact and in handling areas of genuine ambiguity in Augustine in ways that emphasize the harmony between the two thought-worlds. The *Periphyseon* was condemned for pantheistic tendencies, perhaps partly through misunderstanding by theologians not acquainted with eastern theologies.

A treatise of Alcuin, *On the Faith of the Holy and Undivided Trinity*, may sum up the concerns and achievements of early medieval Latin theology. Written partly as a response to the Adoptionist controversy, it is a three-book summary of the Catholic faith, admired and copied in all succeeding centuries up to the advent of printing. It is mostly derivative, consisting of often lengthy passages from the fathers, unattributed and sometimes merged directly with passages drawn from other sources or with sentences in which Alcuin himself speaks. It is thus a work of synthesis and harmonization. It is certainly too strong to say that it is the creation of tradition. But, while concerned to preserve the very language of the fathers as authoritative and not to innovate beyond them, it nevertheless subordinates all their individual voices in its attempt to find its own voice and to articulate precisely what the authoritative tradition of the fathers is saying. In this attempt, it is a true antecedent of the scholastics of the high Middle Ages.

Chadwick, H., *The Early Church* (1967).
di Berardino, A., *Encyclopedia of the Early Church* (1992).
Evans, G. E., *Philosophy and Theology in the Middle Ages* (1993).
Frend, W. H. C., *The Rise of Christianity* (1984).
Ganz, D., *Corbie in the Carolingian Renaissance* (1990).
Hall, S., *Doctrine and Practice in the Early Church* (1991).
Jedin, H., *A History of the Church* (1964; 1980), ii–iii.
Kelly, J. N. D., *Early Christian Doctrines* (1978).
Knowles, D., *The Evolution of Medieval Thought* (1962).
Marenbon, J., *From the Circle of Alcuin to the School of Auxerre* (1981).
Pelikan, J., *The Emergence of the Catholic Tradition (100–600)* (1971).
—— *The Growth of Medieval Theology (600–1000)* (1978).
Quasten, J. *Patrology* (4 vols.; 1950–86).
Southern, R., *Western Society and the Church in the Middle Ages* (1970).

VIII

STRUCTURE AND SANCTITY
The Middle Ages

C. H. Lawrence

BESIDES A RICH LITERARY AND LITURGICAL LEGACY, the Christianity of late antiquity made two particular bequests to the medieval church: *Romanitas*, the culture of classical Rome, and monasticism. Both profoundly influenced its institutional development and permeated its spiritual life.

The most conspicuous heir to the Roman tradition was the pope, the bishop of the ancient capital of the west. After the lapse of a Byzantine imperial presence in Italy, the papacy remained the repository of the imperial idea until it materialized in a new, very different, western empire: in 800 Pope Leo III conferred an imperial crown on Charlemagne, king of the Franks, inaugurating the Christian empire of the Middle Ages under Germanic leadership. The papal claim to dispose of the empire, ignoring Byzantium's claim to be the authentic successor of Rome, was supported by a tradition that Constantine had, in quitting Italy for his eastern capital, conferred on Pope Sylvester I the imperial regalia with dominion over the western empire. In the 8th century, partly to counter Byzantium's claims over Italy, the legend was committed to writing in what pretended to be an imperial diploma.

The legend of Constantine's 'donation' enjoyed a long life, but the hierocratic claims of the medieval papacy to temporal authority over Christendom's rulers rested upon a deeper basis. It derived not from the imperial status of Rome but from the foundation of the Roman see by Peter, to whom Christ entrusted the keys of the kingdom of heaven: a unique commission to teach, protect, and govern the Lord's flock. The bishop of Rome was Peter's successor and heir to his office. In medieval eyes this unique spiritual authority was reinforced by the Roman church's possession of the body of Peter, whose shrine, in the basilica Constantine had built over it, was a focus of pilgrimage from all over Christendom.

In the early Middle Ages veneration for the Apostolic See existed without support from any governmental organization. Men went to Rome, 'threshold of the Apostles', as pilgrims or petitioners, and came back with books and relics. Occasionally they appealed to the pope to vindicate their doctrine or defend their episcopal rights, as they had in antiquity. Following a precedent set by the southern English church, planted by missionaries dispatched by Pope Gregory the Great, archbishops sought papal ratification of their appointment and collected the *pallium* from St Peter's tomb. Otherwise the northern churches did not look to Rome for government or direction. The work of evangelizing northern Europe and creating bishoprics proceeded under the direction of local missionaries and princes. As yet the papacy lacked any administrative apparatus through which it could oversee the affairs of local churches.

The Gregorian Reform movement of the 11th century initiated an expansion of papal government that, over time, transformed the western church into a centralized monarchy under a uniform system of canon law. This movement, inaugurated by Leo IX (1048–54) and brought to a climax by the radical programme of Gregory VII (1073–85), was a reaction against the widespread secularization of ecclesiastical office. Its object was to renew the church by restoring what the reformers regarded as the proper hierarchical order of Christian society, found, they believed, in the primitive church. This involved exalting the priestly office, as having the task of directing God's people to their eternal salvation, and repressing the claims of secular authorities to a voice in spiritual matters. The church was to be

rescued from the abuses of lay control symbolized by the designation and investiture of bishops by lay princes. Zealous bishops
would be chosen through a process of 'free and canonical
election' by the clergy of the church concerned. High on the
agenda was the exaltation of the Apostolic See and the assertion
of its right and duty, implicit in the Petrine commission, to oversee and direct the life of the universal church.

The plan required the creation of a disciplined clergy, conscious of their sacred calling, protected by immunity from the
jurisdiction of the secular courts, and following a way of life that
would detach them from lay preoccupations and distractions. To
this end, the reformers revived the canons of late antiquity for-
bidding marriage to those who served the altar. Clerical marriage,
common in the early Middle Ages, came under mounting attack.
A series of Roman councils decreed that celibacy was required of
clergy in the major orders of priest, deacon, and subdeacon. The
rule was made absolute by the first Lateran Council (1123): no clerk
in major orders could contract a valid marriage. Enforcement of
the law was necessarily slow and difficult; at the level of the rural
parish clergy it never achieved more than partial success.
Although it fell short of turning the clergy into a sacred caste,
it had profound legal and social consequences for medieval
church and society.

In the 12th and 13th centuries, the Gregorian Reform was pro-
moted by a variety of agents, including papal legates dispatched to
regional churches and a series of ecumenical councils, culminating in the fourth Lateran (1215) summoned by Pope Innocent III. It
legislated on a wide range of religious observances, ecclesiastical
discipline, and eradication of abuses. But the main vehicle
through which the post-Gregorian papacy established its supremacy over the entire western church was canon law.

In response to Gregory VII's demand for restoration of the
'ancient law', meaning the order and discipline of the early church,
fresh collections of the early canons were compiled, culminating
in Gratian's *Concordance of Discordant Canons*, c.1140. Combining a systematic collection of early texts with legal discussion, it became at

once a standard text for commentary in the Bologna law schools and laid the foundation of a new science of canon law. It was subsequently supplemented and updated by official collections of later papal decretals. The texts established the pope as supreme lawgiver. As heir of St Peter, he was the 'universal ordinary'— everyman's bishop, to whose tribunal all, however humble, might have access—and the ultimate source from whom the spiritual jurisdiction of his brother bishops was derived.

The consequences of the doctrine of papal sovereignty were inexorably realized in the later Middle Ages and beyond. Papal supremacy materialized in a multitude of ways: an ever-growing flood of petitioners to the papal Curia, taxation of clerical incomes, and papal provision to benefices, a practice extended by the Avignon popes of the 14th century to bishoprics and archbishoprics, thus effectively extinguishing the electoral rights of cathedral chapters. Adopted for fiscal reasons, the practice generally accommodated the wishes of lay rulers, whose nomination of bishops was usually accepted. Thus, in the three centuries after Gregory VII, the western church was welded into a single juridical organism with a centralized government. The Roman Curia developed into a complex bureaucracy. Papal administration was shared by the cardinals, the original archpriests and deacons of the city who, with the bishops of the seven suburbican sees nearest to Rome, came to be recognized in the 11th century as a collegiate body entrusted with the election of the pope. This elaborate structure survived the removal of the Curia to Avignon from 1305 to 1377, when French domination of the Sacred College posed a threat to the international status of the papacy, and emerged intact from the Great Schism (1384–1429), when rival popes contended for the allegiance of Christendom, stimulating the development of conciliarism. It remains essentially that of the Roman Catholic church today.

One aspect of the mental and structural changes produced by the Gregorian papacy was the hardening of polemic between the Latin church and the Greek Orthodox churches of the east. Differences in language, liturgy, and culture widened the separation

of Rome from Constantinople, and in the 11th century controversy arose over the *filioque*—the procession of the Holy Spirit
from the Son—which western tradition had added to the Nicene
creed. The dispute was embittered by a collision between the
Greek and Latin churches in southern Italy and by the uncom-
promising claims of the papacy to universal sovereignty. An
embassy led by the overbearing Cardinal Humbert, sent to Constantinople in 1054 to resolve points of conflict, ended disastrously
with the legates excommunicating the Greek patriarch, Michael
Cerularius, and the legates in turn being excommunicated by the
Greek synod. Subsequent efforts to heal the schism led, after long
negotiation, to public affirmations of unity at the Second Council
of Lyons (1274) and the Council of Florence (1439), but because
they were accepted by the Greek emperors for reasons of political
expediency, with no general support from the eastern clergy, they
proved ephemeral.

One of antiquity's most formative bequests to medieval
Christianity was monasticism. Originating in Egypt and Syria, it
was transmitted to the west both in its eremitical form, derived
from the example of the desert hermits, and in its cenobitical
form of organized ascetical communities. In the 6th century
the monastic ideal received its classical western exposition in
the Rule of St Benedict, which gradually gained acceptance
until in the Carolingian age, with the help of imperial patronage
from Charlemagne and Louis the Pious, it came to be regarded as
the norm of western monastic observance. In the centuries that
followed, the great abbeys, nurseries of saintly bishops and
scholars like Anselm and Bernard of Clairvaux, established a cultural hegemony over the collective mentality of Christian society.
Their intellectual leadership was reinforced by the fact that monastic scriptoria possessed a near monopoly of book-production
until the rise of university stationers at the beginning of the 13th
century.

The spiritual impulse that moved not only princes but people
of every rank to endow religious communities was a desire to
associate themselves with the round of liturgical prayer forming

the framework of the monastic day. The impulse derived its force
from the doctrines of vicarious merit and satisfaction. The notion
of satisfaction to be rendered for sin was fostered by the practice
of private auricular confession and the use of penitentials: these
listed a tariff of penances for every sin, involving fasting and other
ascetical exercises to be performed for a specified number of days,
weeks, or even years, according to the gravity of the sin. The bur-
den of these fearsome documents long haunted the practice of
the confessional, but from the 10th century it was increasingly
alleviated by indulgences—commutation by bishops of specified
periods of canonical penance for prayers, almsgiving, pilgrimage,
or other recognized good works. Indulgences came to hold an
important place in the popular piety of the late Middle Ages.

These features of the penitential system explain the eagerness
of the landed classes to found and endow monasteries. Monks
were 'the poor of Christ', renouncing all personal possessions to
follow the Lord. Supporting them could remit a long period of
penance. More important, through their penitential life of fasting
and prayer they acted as surrogates for their benefactor, perform-
ing satisfaction on his behalf, which, as a deathless society, they
would always continue to do. For many centuries assumptions
about the nature of the Christian life were dominated by monastic theology. From Cassian to St Bernard, the monastic ideal of
renunciation and withdrawal from the world was presented as the
perfect realization of the gospel counsels, indeed the only authentic model of the Christian life. In a world that seemed irremedi-
ably sinful, the cloister offered the only sure path to salvation.
'Acknowledging the enormity of my sins', runs a charter of the
11th century, 'and fearing the dread condemnation of the repro-
bate, I fly to the harbour of safety.' The harbour referred to was
Cluny, then approaching the zenith of its grandeur and influence,
with hundreds of dependent abbeys and priories. Arnaldus, the
charter's author, donated both the church he owned and himself
to Cluny, where he proposed to take the habit. For others, oppressed by the need to do penance, but unable thus to commit
themselves, the best hope of salvation seemed to lie in sharing in

the merits of a monastic community through admission to confraternity—a privilege much sought by both clerical and lay benefactors.

The consensus that monastic life provided the sole paradigm of Christian perfection was reinforced by the images of sanctity disseminated by hagiography—apart from martyrs, most saints in the calendar of the church were prelates or monks. But the monastic ideal was challenged and slowly deprived of its exclusive validity by changes overtaking the church and the whole western world in the 12th century.

An urban renaissance, driven by population growth and expansion of international trade and industry, produced a more affluent and more mobile society. New forms of religious life arose in response, some of them the outcome of tensions within the monastic world itself. At the same time, an exuberant scholastic movement centred in cities, culminating in the creation of the first universities at Bologna, Paris, and Oxford, transferred intellectual leadership from the cloister to the schools of the secular clergy.

A feature of this more complex society was the spread of literacy among lay people, engendering a new kind of spirituality. The idea of vicarious merit dependent upon the prayers of professional ascetics was unsatisfactory for an articulate town-dwelling laity in search of personal religion. One aspect of the religious enthusiasm of this time was the dualist heresy of the Cathars, whose élite combined a life of poverty and rigorous asceticism with itinerant preaching. Although Catharism, with its rejection of the flesh and its repudiation of the Catholic sacraments, bore a resemblance to early Manichaeism, modern scholarship gives more importance to the failings of orthodox teaching than to oriental influence in fostering the heresy. By the middle of the 12th century it had won the allegiance of significant numbers of people in the Languedoc and in the towns of northern and central Italy. It posed the most formidable challenge to the church's spiritual authority until the Hussite rebellion of the 15th century.

Religious toleration was not considered a virtue by the medieval church or by society at large. Religious dissent endangered not only the soul. Since church and state were two arms of the same body, heresy was an attack on the polity, and it was the recognized duty of rulers to repress it. This consensus underlay the draconian penalties decreed against heretics by 13th-century rulers. It was the bishops' duty to detect heretics and delate the unrepentant to the secular power for capital punishment by burning. The spread of Catharism and the failure of local bishops to cope with it persuaded Pope Innocent III to invoke a crusade of the northern knighthood against the Languedoc to depose Count Raymond of Toulouse, who had protected the heretics; and in the 1230s Gregory IX set up the papal inquisition—special commissioners, independent of the local hierarchy, whose task was to investigate those suspected of heresy and persuade them to recant. The few who proved obdurate were to be handed over to the lay power.

Out of the spiritual ferment of the 12th century arose new kinds of religious organization, answering the desire of lay people for active Christian discipleship. Such were the Humiliati, a devout penitential fraternity, with many adherents in the cities of Lombardy and the Veneto, and the group of mendicant lay preachers founded by Waldes, a rich cloth merchant and banker of Lyons. A common inspiration of these movements was the model of the primitive community described in the Acts of the Apostles, epitomized by the term *vita apostolica*, 'the apostolic life'. Monastic tradition had long invoked this to justify the cenobitical life of monks; but now the term acquired a fresh and dynamic meaning. The true apostolic life involved not withdrawal from the world, but engagement with it; its authentic marks were voluntary poverty modelled on the poverty of Christ, mission to the unconverted, and service to the poor. The idea was exemplified by the Breton Robert of Abrissel, who abandoned his clerical career to become a homeless wandering preacher and gathered a throng of disciples, mostly women, in the forests of Maine.

This model of the apostolic life found enthusiastic converts among both the secular clergy and the literate laity. For lay people it offered an ideal of sanctity and a programme that could be realized, without abandoning marriage or worldly responsibilities, in the penitential confraternities that appeared in many Italian towns. These groups, organized and run by lay people, combined a devout life of prayer and ascetical discipline with works of charity. The idea came to its ultimate fruition in the orders of mendicant friars that sprang up in the first decade of the 13th century. The two first and greatest both had discernible roots in the 12th-century ideology of the apostolic life. The Franciscans or Friars Minor originated in the literal and uncomplicated vision of a layman. The Dominicans or Order of Preachers were founded by a Spanish Augustinian canon, and their internal regime bore the stamp of their monastic origin. But both represented a revolutionary departure from monastic tradition by abandoning the principle of enclosure to pursue an active preaching apostolate among the people, and by rejecting corporate ownership of property. Both wrote the ideal of evangelical poverty into their statutes and relied for support upon organized begging.

This new version of the religious life deeply affected the way people thought about the Christian vocation. No subsequent religious order could escape its influence. During the 13th century, this observance was imitated by the Carmelites and Augustinian hermits and other new orders of friars; houses of Mendicants were established in practically every European town. The enthusiasm with which they were welcomed and supported by rulers and townspeople throughout Europe showed that they embodied an idea whose time had come: that it was possible for a committed disciple of Christ to be in the world, but not of it, that the proper condition of those who aspired to spiritual perfection was one of voluntary poverty, and that the imitation of Christ involved an active mission of evangelization either by preaching or personal witness and service to the poor.

To lay people dissatisfied with their role as passive spectators of religious observances and hungry for guidance in personal religion, the friars offered a new theology of the secular life: personal sanctification was within the reach of people in secular trades and professions, even merchants, whose occupation was generally censured by monastic theologians. This new optimism was the directing principle of a new genre of sermon in which the friars excelled, sermons *ad status*, addressed to the spiritual needs of different classes and occupations: sermons for knights, merchants, scholars, masters and servants, rulers, and married people, taking full account of their state and responsibilities. The devout lay person took his or her place alongside the monk and the secular priest as an authentic Christian.

The friars' first century was a turning-point in the history of popular piety. An intense devotion to the humanity of Christ, a concern with the details of his earthly life, and a compassionate regard for his sufferings were features of a new orientation of western religious sentiment that had its roots in the monastic spirituality of the 12th century. Compassion or imaginative identification with the sufferings of Jesus was an important theme in the writings of St Bernard and the Cistercians. It was largely through the teaching of the Franciscans that in the 13th century it emerged from the cloister and became a central theme in the religious experience of the ordinary Christian. Francis himself became the supreme example, his experience validated by the imprint on his body of the stigmata of the crucified Christ. This change in people's intuitive and emotional response to the story of redemption was expressed in such popular devotions as the crib, the rosary, and the Office of the Passion. It was also reflected in western art. In the century separating Bernard from Bonaventure, the passionless triumphant Christ of Romanesque art is replaced by the contorted figure of the Man of Sorrows hanging on the cross.

One of the major services the friars rendered the church was their contribution to education. The medieval church never devised institutions to train the secular clergy outside the annual meetings of the diocesan synod. The majority of parish clergy were recruited locally from the free peasantry; and, apart from an educated élite absorbed by the schools and ecclesiastical administration, their education was barely above that of their rustic parishioners. The diocesan seminary was an invention of the 16th century. This gap in the pastoral equipment of the church was filled by the friars. Recognizing that a mission to the articulate people of the towns, especially those touched by the Cathar heresy, required theological education and mental agility, they created a scholastic system of their own. Every friary had a classroom, where the brethren were taught by a lector and practised the art of disputation. Their ablest pupils proceeded to schools of their order in the universities, where they succeeded so brilliantly that their teaching and written works dominated the study of western theology for more than a century. By opening their schools to outsiders, the mendicants also made a significant contribution to improving the educational standards of the parish clergy.

The 12th-century intellectual renaissance took many forms and flowed into many channels, but at its heart was the recovery of a great part of Graeco-Arabic philosophy and science, through Latin translation and the revived study of classical Roman law. In the course of the century these discoveries revolutionized both the content and methods of learning. Aristotle's works on logic, metaphysics, and natural science, and his Arab commentators, confronted scholars with a new world of scientific knowledge and speculation, seeming to offer for the first time the possibility of a rational understanding of the physical universe and the place of man in relation to God and the moral order. If not everything was known or even knowable, everything was at least intelligible in principle and open to rational enquiry, including God's plan for humankind as revealed in the person of Jesus Christ. The scholastic method consisted of the application of dialectic or analytic logic to the study of authoritative texts. The status of recognized authorities rested upon the premiss that the teacher's task was to recover the lost wisdom of the ancients. As Bernard of Chartres told his pupils, 'we are pygmies standing upon the shoulders of giants', a dictum illustrated for posterity by the 13th-century glass-maker of the south transept of Chartres Cathedral, who depicted the evangelists seated on the shoulders of the gigantic prophets of the OT. Every discipline had its recognized authorities. The law doctors of Bologna lectured on the *Code* and *Digest* of Justinian, the canonists on Gratian and the later papal decretals.

For theologians, the authoritative text was the Latin Vulgate bible, and the fundamental task was the exegesis of the inspired text. With the advance of theological inquiry in the Paris schools, stimulated by the teaching of Abelard, an additional prescribed authority was found in the *Sentences* of Peter Lombard, a coherent conspectus of Christian doctrine, providing a more systematic treatment of doctrinal questions than was possible within the framework of the biblical lecture. The use of the *Sentences* as a course-book was pioneered by the friars teaching theology at Paris in the years 1230-45. Peter Lombard's book made possible the rise of theology as a science, based upon the rational exploration of the data of revelation. It paved the way for the great *summas*—the systematic compendia of doctrinal questions composed by leading schoolmen like Alexander of Hales, Albert of Cologne, and Aquinas.

For several centuries scholasticism was a bond uniting an international community of learning in a common enterprise. In universities throughout western Europe schoolmen studied the same texts and debated in a common scholastic idiom. Their aim was the enlargement of man's understanding of his place in the universe through rational enquiry. It was an enterprise with severe limitations in the field of physical science: the Ptolemaic model of a universe of geocentric spheres would not be superseded in popular consciousness until the 17th century; but scholasticism gave to western theology and canon law much of their conceptual framework. Its language and concepts continued to dominate the discourse of both Catholic and Protestant polemicists during the Reformation and beyond.

The impact of scholastic thought was evident in several forms of religious observance in the later Middle Ages. One was devotion to the 'real presence' of Christ in the mass, focused especially upon the elevation of the host following the words of institution. This devotion, which found expression in Corpus Christi guilds and public processions as well as in private worship, was inspired by the scholastic concept of transubstantiation—the use of Aristotelian categories to elucidate the eucharistic mystery—given formal approval by the Lateran Council of 1215. Another preoccupation of late medieval piety inspired by scholastic theology was a concern with purgatory. The Paris schoolmen of the 13th century clarified and defined the inchoate belief of earlier ages in a state of purgation after death, involving transitory suffering, which could be alleviated by the suffrages of the living. This belief inspired innumerable private devotions as well as the Office of the Dead, masses, charitable bequests, and chantry foundations.

More than is commonly appreciated, lay piety of the Middle Ages was nourished by scripture. The immense cost and time involved in medieval book-production precluded the possession of a complete bible. The popular one-volume bible was an invention of printing. Individual books and sections, such as the Pentateuch, the gospels, and the Pauline epistles, were used in the schools and circulated more widely. Daily use of the psalter was common among literate lay people of both sexes. In response to the growth of lay literacy in the 12th century, translations of the gospels and epistles began to appear in French and Provençal, and Anglo-Norman versions appeared in England. The Augsburg Bible of 1350 provided a High German translation of the whole NT. In 14th-century England, Middle-English versions of the bible made by John Wyclif's followers, being tainted by the Wyclifite heresy, drew from Archbishop Arundel the first official condemnation of unauthorized translations of scripture. But both vernacular and Latin versions of the psalms and the Passion narratives continued to circulate ever more widely in the primers or books of hours. Vernacular versions of the 12th-century *Historia Scholastica* of Peter Comestor, one of the most influential of the Paris schoolmen, disseminated knowledge of the events and figures of the OT.

Although from the 11th century onwards an increasing body of vernacular literature was aimed at the needs and tastes of women, who shared in the spread of literacy among the upper classes and the urban bourgeoisie, women had no part in the scholastic movement of the 12th and 13th centuries. In accordance with the tradition it received from antiquity, the secular church of the Middle Ages excluded them from any official role. Not only sacramental acts but all ecclesiastical functions, including teaching, were confined to men. By contrast, women had filled a conspicuous role in the monastic church. In the Germanic world of Merovingian Gaul and Anglo-Saxon England, their high status was reflected in their prominence as monastic founders and royal abbesses of nunneries and double monasteries ruling both men and women with the self-assurance that was their birthright. Abbesses, including Hilda of Whitby and Gertrude of Nivelles, were among the most influential religious leaders of their generation. But in the aristocratic society of the 11th and 12th centuries, where legal arrangements and modes of thought were conditioned by the military fief, women were reduced to a subordinate role. They played no part in the initiatives that launched new monastic movements like Cîteaux and Prémontré. Similarly, ecclesiastical tradition and social convention denied an active role to the women devotees of the *vita apostolica* and the mendicant ideals of the 13th century, so that the female branches of the Franciscan and Dominican friars were strictly enclosed, contemplative orders of a traditional monastic type. Nevertheless, both the Beguine movement and the 'third orders' linked with the friars provided space for women in and after the 13th century to be committedly 'religious' yet unenclosed. Within the constrictions of monastic institutions, and more often outside them, women had always figured among the leading mystics and teachers of the contemplative life. In the crises that afflicted the church of the later Middle Ages, some, like the Beguine Marie d'Oignies and the Dominican tertiary, Catherine of Siena, emerged as solitary prophets, exerting a decisive influence upon the ecclesiastical leaders of their time.

In a multitude of ways the thought and experience of the medieval centuries have left their impress upon the Christianity of the modern world. The medieval structure of ecclesiastical government and law has shaped the institutions of all episcopal churches. The writings of the medieval mystics and speculative theologians continue to nourish religious sentiment and spirituality transcending all confessional boundaries. Besides compelling paradigms of sanctity, the Middle Ages bequeathed to Christendom a huge treasury of liturgical prayer in the eucharistic liturgies and the eightfold daily offices, traces of which are clearly visible in all service-books, Protestant as well as Catholic, that derive from the medieval tradition.

Brooke, C. N. L., *The 12th-Century Renaissance* (1969).

Chenu, M.-D., *Nature, Man and Society in the Twelfth Century*, ET (1968).

Dvornik, F., *Byzantium and the Roman Primacy* (1966).

Knowles, M. D., *The Monastic Order in England* (1949).

Lambert, M., *Medieval Heresy: Popular Movements from Bogomil to Hus* (1977).

Lawrence, C. H., *Medieval Monasticism: Forms of Religious Life in Western Europe in the Middle Ages*, 2nd edn. (1989).

—— *The Friars: The Impact of the Mendicant Movement on Western Society* (1994).

Leclercq, J., Vandenbrucke, F., and Bouyer, L., *The Spirituality of the Middle Ages: A History of Spirituality* (1968), ii.

Little, L. K., *Religious Poverty and the Profit Economy in Medieval Europe* (1978).

Moore, R. I., *The Origins of European Dissent*, 2nd edn. (1985).

Renouard, Y., *The Avignon Papacy*, ET (1970).

Smalley, Beryl, *The Study of the Bible in the Middle Ages*, 3rd edn. (1983).

Southern, R. W., *St Anselm and his Biographer* (1963).

—— *Western Society and the Church in the Middle Ages* (1970).

—— *Scholastic Humanism and the Unification of Europe* (1995).

Tellenbach, G., *Church, State and Christian Society at the Time of the Investiture Contest*, 3rd edn. (1989).

Vauchez, A., *La Sainteté en occident aux derniers siècles du moyen-age* (1984).

Ullmann, W., *A Short History of the Papacy in the Middle Ages* (1972).

—— *The Growth of Papal Government in the Middle Ages* (1955).

IX

DIVERSITY AND ORTHODOXY
The 16th century

❧ + ❧

Seán F. Hughes

OST PEOPLE HAVE INHERITED VESTIGIAL STORIES of what happened to western Christianity in the early modern era. Often these take the form of either rejection of 'Roman' errors and uncovering of gospel truth by Protestants, or rebellion against Catholic orthodoxy by Protestant renegades and defence of the true faith by those remaining in communion with the Apostolic See. To transcend narrow denominational accounts and achieve a balanced assessment remains a major challenge. While pure hermeneutical disinterestedness is impossible to achieve, significant strides have been made by historians and ecumenical theologians in overcoming polemical distortion, and many scholars are looking anew at the interaction of various theologies in the late 15th and 16th centuries, avoiding the caricatures and simplistic dichotomies of the past.

The wealth and diversity of theological movements in western Europe at this time can seem bewildering. This article aims to give a sense of the main issues dividing Catholics and mainstream Protestants, and of the principal ways in which central perceptions in Christianity changed and fragmented. It traces the origins and development of the three major communities that dominated western Europe by the end of the 16th century, Catholics, Lutherans, and the Reformed, and surveys the major doctrinal themes of the era: grace, the sacraments, ministry, the church, and the correct use of the bible and the writings of early and medieval divines. The theological importance of radical groups, Protestant and otherwise, is not to be underestimated, but because of their numerous divisions and the complex spectrum of views to be found within them, they are treated here only in relation to Catholic and mainstream Protestant positions.

The period from *c.*1470 to *c.*1600 was one of immense intellectual fertility. Seminal developments were made in numerous areas, many of which, principally because of the marginalization of theology as an intellectual discipline, now seem remote from the work of the theologian: for example, the theories of the Tübingen theology professor, Gabriel Biel (*c.*1420–95), concerning the nature of money, or the work of the Spaniards, Francisco de Vitoria (*c.*1485–1546) and Francisco de Suarez (1548–1617) on international law. Many late-medieval and early-modern Christian writers paid considerable attention to fields, such as cabbalism, hermeticism, and astrology, that strike the modern reader as bizarre. In addition theologians were profoundly affected by and were often the instigators of radical change in linguistic, textual, and critical scholarship. Nor did they hold aloof as the dissemination of knowledge was revolutionized by the invention of printing. A large proportion of books printed by the end of the 15th century were theological or devotional, including numerous editions of the bible, both in Latin and in various vernaculars.

In the popular mind the 16th century is associated with the Protestant Reformation. Yet there was not *one* Reformation, but a number of interrelated but distinct Reformations, including very importantly a *Catholic* Reformation. Calls for reform of the church had been widespread in the 15th century, but with no consensus on what needed to be reformed. Contrary to some traditional views that the late-medieval church was in a state of terminal decay and unable to satisfy spiritual needs, recent work on the English church on the eve of the Reformation suggests that parish religion in many parts of the country was vibrant and robust. This complex and luxuriant structure of liturgy and piety was, at least in England, extremely successful in sustaining and communicating particular central truths of medieval Christianity about the bonds of charity binding the living with the living, and the living with the dead. It is difficult to know how far this analysis applies beyond England. While religion on a micro-level may have been in a healthy state, at the macro-level of dioceses, regions, nations, and the international church the situation looked much less rosy: excesses, sanctioned and unsanctioned, in popular piety, distortions of fundamental doctrines, theological confusion, and numerous clerical abuses. Perhaps the late medieval church's very vitality made its flaws all the more glaring.

One practice that certainly required reform was the issue of indulgences. Despite apparently clear official teaching that indulgences were only remissions of the *temporal* punishment for sins already pardoned by God, and that the church could not automatically apply these benefits to those in purgatory, grotesque distortions and misunderstandings were widely current at the beginning of the 16th century. What is astonishing is that the break-up of western Christianity should be initiated through the publication of a highly technical list of propositions for academic disputation on the subject by an obscure German university professor: Martin Luther's Ninety-Five Theses (1517). The Theses not only called for reform of indulgences, but presented a radical critique of central elements of medieval religion underpinning the practice. Luther's excommunication did not end the controversy, which released a torrent of reforming zeal and soul-searching throughout Western Europe after almost a century of frustrated expectations of reform. By 1520 Luther had spelled out his radical rejection of the hierarchical church and priesthood, the dominant theologies of grace and the system of the seven sacraments, proposing instead a priesthood of all believers, freedom for Christians from 'earning' salvation, and the two sacraments of the gospel, baptism and holy communion, with penance, at least in the early stages, retaining a semi-sacramental status. How would the church as a whole respond?

Pope Leo X had condemned Luther's teachings using all the force of papal authority, but his bull did not have the desired effect, indicating the lack of consensus in the church on who should ultimately arbitrate in such disputes. There seemed to be a considerable chasm between the papacy's elevated spiritual claims and its more mundane reality: until the reforming popes of the mid-16th century the bishops of Rome often appeared more like Italian princes than 'servants of the servants of God'. Pope Leo seemed unable to bring about the necessary reform of the church. Nor had the Fifth Lateran Council (1512–17) done so. Yet Luther appealed for adjudication to a truly free ecumenical synod. The bull *Execrabilis* (1460) of Pope Pius II condemning appeals from a pope to a future general council had failed to eradicate widespread, if inchoate, conciliarist ideas, particularly the prestige possessed by the initial decrees of the Council of Constance. Much uncertainty remained about the limits of papal authority; the question of the ultimate superiority of an ecumenical council over the papacy was not definitively settled in Catholic circles during the 16th century. Fear of the threat to papal authority posed by a general council, and the papacy's complex political entanglements, meant that Rome did not call a reforming council until 1537. It did not meet until 1545 at Trent. Its sessions were so frequently interrupted by tensions between the papacy and the Catholic powers that Trent did not end formally until 1563.

The residual conciliarism of the 16th century was only one element of the complex medieval inheritance concerning authority in the church. Although the papacy had repeatedly tried to impose a straightforward papal monarchy, medieval Catholicism had never accepted that there was just one locus of authority in the church. Authority remained much more diffused than the papacy wished. The church had to acknowledge the authority not only of popes, cardinals, the Curia, councils, and metropolitan synods, but frequently that of charismatic reforming figures and movements. Sometimes these succeeded and stayed within the bounds of the church, as did Catherine of Siena or the Observant movements in various religious orders; sometimes they failed, as did Girolamo Savonarola (1452–98). Luther appeared to many as just such a prophetic figure. There was also the controverted 'teaching authority' of academic theologians: an important example is the central, sometimes independent, role played by the Theology Faculty of the University of Paris in the defence of orthodoxy and the condemnation of Luther and other 'heretics'.

In many minds the Reformation is intimately connected with 'humanism'. Humanism in the late 15th and 16th centuries was not a unified ideology with a particular perspective on religion, but a collection of new educational techniques: innovative modes of argumentation emphasizing the importance of style and rhetoric, bypassing commentators, ancient and medieval, to return 'to the sources' of ancient pagan and Christian learning, and hence a renewed interest in early Christian writings, especially the text of scripture. Erasmus' Greek NT is justly famous, but humanist biblical scholarship was not the preserve of critics of the institutional church: the Complutensian Polyglot produced in Spain under Cardinal Ximénez de Cisneros must not be overlooked. Although Catholics did become more defensive about the authoritativeness of the Vulgate because of radical humanist and, later, Protestant attacks on its reliability, Catholic scholars remained deeply committed to the study of the Hebrew OT and the Greek OT and NT. While some humanists, like Erasmus, were very critical of scholastic theology's barbarous Latin, cumbersome organization of arguments, and supposed obsession with distinctions, there was no necessary opposition between scholasticism and humanism. John Fisher, executed for refusing to accept Henry VIII's supremacy in the Church of England, and one of the forces behind the introduction of humanist techniques into Cambridge University, used the full resources of scholastic theology against Lutheran 'errors'.

Humanistic techniques brought about changes in scholastic theology itself. One of Luther's earliest opponents, Cardinal Cajetan (Tomaso de Vio, 1469–1534), began to write commentaries, not on Peter Lombard's *Sentences*, the almost universal late-medieval practice, but on Aquinas's writings, especially his more mature works. Rather than any decline of scholasticism in the 16th century, a massive flowering took place, particularly in the Spanish universities where scholasticism and Thomism became so linked that the terms are often treated as synonyms. While their Latin style may still have aroused humanists' ire, Spanish scholastics enthusiastically adopted many humanist critical and historical techniques. Like Erasmus, first- and second-generation Protestant Reformers railed against the evils of scholasticism, but even within the second generation some took a different view; and by the last quarter of the century various scholasticisms, invigorated by the synthesis with humanism, came to dominate Lutheran and Reformed academic theology. Although humanist methods did not necessarily result in particular religious perspectives, leading figures like Erasmus (who never formally broke with Rome) were vehement advocates of reform in the church. The term 'evangelical' is often used to describe groups arising in the late 1510s, 1520s, and 1530s in response to the ferment of reformist ideas, inspired by the scripturalism and piety espoused by Erasmus and others. By no means all attached to such circles, like that around Guillaume Briçonnet (c.1470–1534), bishop of Meaux, were proto-Protestants. It is difficult to establish convincing patterns explaining why this or that humanist did or did not become Protestant. Two prominent cardinals, who had been profoundly affected by the Christocentric scripturalism of Italian 'evangelism', were investigated on suspicion of holding Lutheran errors: Reginald Pole, appointed a presiding legate for the Council of Trent, almost elected pope in 1549, archbishop of Canterbury and architect of the Catholic Reformation in England under Mary I; and Giovanni Morone, also at one time a candidate for the papacy, a papal diplomat, and presiding legate at several Tridentine sessions.

A renewed emphasis on the centrality of scripture was part of both Catholic and Protestant Reformations, but mainstream Protestants characterized their position with the term 'scripture alone'. The principle was often applied at face value by radical groups, but magisterial Protestants were at times surprisingly 'traditional'. They defended infant baptism against Anabaptists, and suppressed those who attacked the doctrine of the Trinity contained in the ancient creeds; Michael Servetus was burned in Calvin's Geneva for his anti-Trinitarianism. Indeed mainstream Protestants like Luther, Zwingli, and Calvin never questioned that the Blessed Virgin Mary was the Mother of God, a title which was an integral part of the christological teaching of the Councils of Ephesus and Chalcedon. They generally accepted the authority of the first four councils, and held the fifth and sixth in high regard. What is more unexpected is their adamant adherence to the much less dogmatically significant perpetual virginity of Mary. It has been argued that the post-Reformation Church of England had a peculiar concern for the authority of the fathers and of medieval writers including Aquinas, to whom the 'Calvinists' and other Continental Protestants supposedly attributed little weight. In fact, both Reformed and Lutherans in the 16th century had as much interest in the early fathers as writers usually construed as 'Anglican'. Not surprisingly, Church of England, as well as other Reformed and Lutheran, theologians rejected the dominant late-medieval teaching (developed largely by canon lawyers, and majority Catholic opinion after Trent) that tradition contained binding doctrine not found in scripture; but they also rejected the early-medieval and High Scholastic view (to which a minority of post-Tridentine Catholic divines adhered) that the content of scripture and of the church's traditional teaching was identical. Instead they held that the writings of the fathers and medieval divines could not provide any normative key to scripture, but were still an important aid in its interpretation and in demonstrating the antiquity of Protestant doctrines.

Later there was a decisive break in the intellectual continuity of mainstream Protestantism, especially among the Reformed, on the issue of scripture and tradition. Reformed confidence in the usefulness of early and medieval writers as authorities waned, due in part to the writings of Jean Daillé (1594–1670). Daillé argued that the purity of apostolic teaching had degenerated very rapidly; that it was impossible to reach a consensus of patristic opinion on crucial issues; and that the fathers' context was so different from that in which Protestants found themselves that patristic views had little relevance to the construction of sound Protestant theology. This marginalizing of patristics may have been partly a delayed response to the increased sophistication of Catholic scholarship on the early church by the third quarter of the century. As some consensus gradually developed on which ancient texts were authentic and which forgeries, Catholic writers could argue persuasively for the antiquity of doctrines and practices objectionable to Protestants, such as prayer for the dead and veneration of saints. This crisis also affected the Church of England, although it is a sign of the parting of the ways with the Reformed that took place in the seventeenth century that some of Daillé's most vehement opponents were English.

The very existence of the collection of documents called the bible was one of the strongest Catholic arguments for authoritative interpretation of scripture by the church; how could one recognize the canon without the witness of the church? Few Protestants were willing to follow Luther in making Christ's gospel (not the gospels) the test of canonicity as he did for the Epistle of James. But the canon also needed careful treatment on the Catholic side. The Council of Trent solemnly declared the complete canonicity of the Hebrew OT, and of the OT books found in Greek and Latin but not in Hebrew; yet it excluded three texts traditionally included in the Vulgate, the Prayer of Manasseh and 3 (1) and 4 (2) Esdras. Earlier, Cajetan had not been alone in advocating the shorter Hebrew canon, and some ambiguity remained implicit in the post-Tridentine distinction between proto- and deutero-canonical books.

Erasmus and many early Protestants had a profound optimism about the clarity of scripture, despite major differences in their exegetical methods. Luther, although he had a flair for innovative scriptural commentary, as in his interpretation of the Pauline concept of justice/righteousness, was quite traditional in his adherence to various forms of allegorical reading. Ironically Cajetan was to cause some shock in traditionalist Catholic circles through his thoroughgoing advocacy of Aquinas's teaching on the primacy of the 'literal sense' of scripture. Naivety about the perspicuity of scripture disappeared rapidly as Protestants confronted the intractability of their own divisions and the even greater threat of radical Protestant exegeses. Although theoretically scripture remained an unnormed norm, in practice Protestant theologians were trained in correct interpretation through an avalanche of catechisms and confessions of faith.

At the heart of Luther's programme was the centrality of God's agency in salvation. This divine prevenience had been defended in the early church by Augustine. Though his doctrines had been clouded by lack of complete versions of his works and by a plethora of forgeries, and although there had never been an official endorsement of his controversial later teachings, it is still fair to say that all western theology since Augustine, including that of the 16th century, operated within an Augustinian framework. Augustinian ideas, if not always the text of his writings, were at the centre of Reformation debates. In the late Middle Ages rigorist Augustinian teachings on grace were not the preserve of radical figures like John Wyclif. An archbishop of Canterbury, Thomas Bradwardine (c.1295–1349), and Gregory of Rimini (c.1300–58), who became the prior general of the Augustinian Hermits, had both vigorously opposed what they perceived as the Pelagianism of many contemporaries. Recent scholarship has emphasized the significance of Gregory and his disciples for the period just before the Reformation. One of the schools suspected of Pelagianism by the 'Augustinians' was that branch of the 'Modern Way' derived from William of Ockham. Its most significant exponent in the late 15th century was Gabriel Biel, who heavily emphasized the human ability to co-operate with divine grace; for him God and human beings were partners in the work of salvation. One of his central axioms was the scholastic tag that God does not deny grace to those who do their best, which led him to hold that human beings were able in a certain sense to merit forgiveness of sins.

Luther's love of paradoxes, such as 'righteous and a sinner at the same time', was part of his attempt to encapsulate the human *experience* of divine forgiveness and union with Christ. Traditional Catholic theological language, before and after Trent, sought rather to express in abstract terms the *state* of being in or out of friendship with God: states which logically could not coexist. There was in Catholicism an unresolved tension between the abstractions of formal theology and the vigorous tradition, especially in Spain, of reflection on the spiritual life. Traditions of mystical prayer were tolerated that did not relativize the church's sacraments and hierarchy through the 'subjectivism' of which certain Spanish 'enlightened ones' (*alumbrados*) were suspected. While Ignatius of Loyola, the founder of the Society of Jesus, had immense devotion to the authority of the institutional church, he successfully defended himself against the Inquisition's questioning of the authenticity and orthodoxy of the mystical experiences that were to form the basis of his *Spiritual Exercises*. John of the Cross and Teresa of Avila faced similar hostility. Yet one of the foremost scholastic theologians of his day, the Dominican Domingo Bañez, was for a time Teresa's confessor and ardent defender. As for mainstream Protestantism, while its first and second generations could confidently proclaim the certitude which the believer should have of being graced, succeeding generations became more divided over the theoretical formulation of this assurance and the problems of its practical application in pastoral situations.

By the second half of the 16th century, Catholic theologians had resolved some of the late-medieval muddle about the human capacity to act virtuously apart from grace, emphasizing that, while fallen human beings could freely perform naturally good acts, they could not, without the assistance of divine grace, perform supernatural acts meriting salvation. For mainstream Protestants, adherence to concepts of merit, however qualified, was at the root of Rome's rottenness: its contamination of the central Christian truth that salvation is by grace alone. Nevertheless Catholic use of 'merit', at least in academic theology, was always within a fundamentally Augustinian framework. The Tridentine decree on justification relativized all such usage when, alluding to Augustine, it stated that God chooses to crown his gifts as our merits.

From the perspective of post-Tridentine Catholic orthodoxy Erasmus, in his controversy with Luther on freedom of the will, was still writing in a 'Pelagian' way; 'semi-Pelagian' was coined in the 16th century to describe the theological fuzziness of writers like Erasmus, deemed to have given excessive weight to human initiative in salvation. But Luther obscured the issue for contemporary and later Catholic readers by his penchant for such hyperbolic expressions as 'the enslaved will'. In the more coherently anti-Pelagian context of late 16th-century Catholicism, Thomists could teach (much closer to Luther than to Erasmus) that God's efficacious grace achieves its end by a necessity of infallibility, not a necessity of coercion: the human will is infallibly yet freely moved by grace. Yet at the end of the century the Jesuit Luis de Molina was developing the novel ideas that human freedom necessarily involved liberty from any external agency, and that God's agency was external. This concept approximates to some modern notions of freedom as autonomy and had radical implications for the doctrine of grace. Thomists in the Dominican order were horrified at what they saw as resurgent semi-Pelagianism attacking the newly formed consensus that Aquinas was the safest guide on such matters. Even Molina's fellow Jesuit, Robert Bellarmine, believed Molina had fallen into grave error. A papal commission, *De Auxiliis* (concerning forms of grace), was appointed in 1597 to examine Molina's orthodoxy and sat intermittently for almost ten years. Several times he only narrowly escaped condemnation, but in the end the commission was dissolved and a stalemate established that lasted until the present day, with the Thomist and 'Molinist' positions both declared tenable.

It is often assumed that the increasing dominance of scholastic modes of thought in Reformed theology distorted Calvin's more moderate doctrine of grace into an extreme form of determinism as introduced by 'supralapsarians' like Theodore Beza (1519–1605) and the internationally renowned Cambridge divine, William Perkins (1558–1602). In fact their teaching, while more speculative than Calvin's, was in important respects more balanced and moderate. Scholastic categories helped to introduce a careful nuancing of which Calvin had disapproved. Moreover, their doctrine of predestination cannot properly be called determinist. The majority of the Reformed, in any case, advocated a doctrine of predestination closer to Thomist and Augustinian Catholic positions, and more nuanced and restrained than that of Beza and his followers. Catholic Thomists and Augustinians needed to distort mainstream Reformed positions in order to differentiate them from their own teaching, saying that whereas they merely taught a 'negative antecedent reprobation', 'Calvinists' taught a 'positive antecedent reprobation'. In fact, most infralapsarians, like Roman supporters of absolute predestination, emphasized that reprobation was a purely negative act, the 'passing over' of those in the damnable lump of humanity whose own demerits justly sent them to hell. Many Catholic and mainstream Reformed doctrines of predestination were thus virtually identical. They differed, not in the doctrines of predestination *per se* but, most significantly, in the Reformed affirmation of the complete identity between the number of the justified and the elect (a doctrine known as the golden chain), with the consequent possibility of a believer's knowing that he or she was justified and *ergo* one of the elect.

The Council of Trent reaffirmed the medieval teaching on the seven sacraments without adjudicating on the numerous disagreements in this area among Catholic theologians. Trent repeated the medieval doctrine that the mass is a propitiatory sacrifice for the living and the dead. Luther and other Protestant theologians rejected this understanding as impinging on the uniqueness and all-sufficiency of Christ's sacrifice. Most late-medieval theologians, like Gabriel Biel, had argued that individual masses, as repetitions of Calvary, did add in some way to the merits of the crucifixion. Similar views remained dominant in 16th-century Catholicism, although a minority, including Cajetan, followed Aquinas in teaching that the mass as a memorial sacrifice is identical with Christ's one sacrifice and gains all its efficacy from it. Luther saw the medieval 'canon' of the mass with its constant reiteration of human offering to God as yet another example of Roman 'works' theology, so he pared it down to what for him was the efficacious proclamation of the gospel's grace, the narrative of the Last Supper. Justification by faith and grace alone had not abolished the crucial significance of the sacraments of baptism and the Eucharist. While Lutherans rejected the medieval notion of the sacraments dispensing grace 'out of the action performed', baptism and 'the sacrament of the altar' remained very much 'means of grace'. Zwingli's radical teaching that the sacraments were essentially mnemonics of grace already given was anathema to Luther. All mainstream Protestants taught that faith was required to enjoy the benefits of God's gifts in these dominical ordinances, but what sense was to be made of the baptism of infants, so vehemently defended against Anabaptists? Luther and many of his disciples, concerned to protect baptism's efficacy, argued for an 'infant faith', notions ridiculed by Zwingli's followers. But others in the Reformed tradition, such as Calvin, did want to affirm, however cautiously, that baptism had present as well as past and future effects.

While baptism continued to be a contentious issue between Lutherans and the Reformed, the Lord's supper became a geological fault line. Luther and his more zealous disciples held doctrines of the real presence of Christ in the Eucharist as far from Zwinglian minimalism as contemporary Roman doctrines of transubstantiation. Lutherans objected to the Catholic doctrine, not because it taught the real presence, but because it had elevated an unscriptural piece of scholastic speculation to the level of dogma. Lutherans never resorted to 'consubstantiation' or 'impanation' to describe their own teaching. All who would not accept the Lutheran shibboleth of 'in, with, and under' the bread and wine, and who did not distance themselves from 'Zwinglianism' were to be condemned. In fact many Reformed found Zwingli's teaching as objectionable as Luther's. Calvin and others taught a real communication of Christ to the believer in the sacrament, but avoided any notion of a 'presence' in the bread and wine. Bullinger in Zurich, while not willing to go as far

as Calvin, was ready to moderate Zwingli's extremism; he and
Calvin achieved an uneasy and ambiguous consensus on eucharistic doctrine among the Reformed.

Central to Lutheranism and indeed all forms of Protestantism, radical and magisterial, was a desire to remove what were
perceived as barriers between the believer and Christ. He was the
one mediator between God and humanity, making all other supposed advocates and mediators unnecessary, whether in heaven
(Mary and the saints), or on earth (the sacrificing priesthood). For
mainstream Protestants, priesthood, other than the priesthood of
all the baptized or of believers, had been abolished. Nevertheless
structure in the church, meaning ministers of some sort,
remained a necessity, either because good order and decency,
and human propensity to sin, required subjection to authority
(the dominant position in Lutheranism, also held by some
Reformed, including many Church of England, theologians), or
because scripture specified the basic elements of church government (the teaching of Calvin and his many disciples). The Swedish
and English Protestant churches kept bishops in the historical
succession, though the Swedes and initially the English attached
no theological significance to them. In the English church the
first defences of episcopacy as 'by divine law' came only towards
the end of the century. It is not surprising that there was confusion over the theology of ministry since medieval ideas had
been so untidy. It was common teaching that bishops did not
form a separate order of minister in the sacrament of orders:
the major orders were usually listed as priests, deacons, and sub-
deacons. Was there an absolute need for bishops? Many seemed
more like bureaucratic administrators or temporal lords than
'successors of the apostles' or pastors of their dioceses. Even
their absolute necessity for ordaining other ministers could be
questioned on the basis of 15th-century papal dispensations to
abbots (who were only presbyters) to perform ordinations. Lutheran princes took on many functions of episcopal oversight
in their territories. Even among the Reformed, Elizabeth I's supreme governorship of the Church of England was not an unpar-

alleled example of Erastianism: the views of Thomas Erastus, vehemently attacked by Genevan theologians, were a defence of the model for church–state relations actually existing in Zurich and Basel, where ultimate authority in disputes between church and state lay with the magistrates. In the Catholic sphere, though the papacy, in theory, regained its authority over the 'eldest daughter of the church' through the Concordat of Bologna (1516), in fact it remained a rubber stamp for the royal control of the French church, ironically well before the schism between Henry VIII's English church and Rome.

All the churches resulting from these Reformations claimed to be 'the Catholic church' of the ancient creeds. Luther, in his vernacular of the Apostles' Creed, went so far as to translate Catholic as Christian, to demonstrate that this venerable epithet had nothing to do with 'the papal church'. Papal church, popery, church of Rome were among the ways opponents referred to those communities which had the most direct institutional, liturgical, and doctrinal continuity with the medieval Catholic church of the west. The doctrinal claim of these communities that the 'one, holy, catholic and apostolic church' on earth was identical with themselves was emphatically asserted, despite opposition from other groups, through their use of 'Catholic' as their own name. The modern usage of 'Roman Catholic' was invented in the 17th century by Protestants as a more polite form for use in diplomatic contexts.

The Lutheran churches derived principally from Luther's theological inspiration, and to a lesser extent from that of his friend and associate, Philip Melanchthon. There seems not to have been much opposition to 'Lutheran' as a colloquial self-designation, except possibly in Scandinavia. By the end of the century Lutherans were mainly found there and in northern Germany, with smaller communities in southern and western Germany, and Eastern Europe, although earlier, before divisions with the Reformed had hardened, adherents were more widely scattered.

More formally, Lutherans referred to themselves in variants of 'Evangelical Christians [or Churches] (of the Confession of

Augsburg)'. The principal author of the original version of the Augsburg Confession (1530), the most widely accepted of Lutheran confessional documents, was Melanchthon. Most Reformed were willing to subscribe to the Confession, but only in an altered form penned by Melanchthon in 1541. He tried to reunite mainstream Protestants through a more ambiguous formulation of the Confession's teaching on the Eucharist. Numerous colloquies failed to bring about reconciliation and, despite Melanchthon's incalculable impact on the Lutheran tradition, a so-called 'genuine' or Gnesio-Lutheran party relentlessly harried his followers as traitors, referring to them as Philippists or Crypto-Calvinists. The promulgation of the Formula of Concord (1577) and the Book of Concord (1580) were largely a victory in Germany for the hardliners. However, the Scandinavian churches continued to emphasize the primacy of the 1530 Confession of Augsburg, reluctant to accept what they perceived as the burdensome obsession with theological precision of their German co-religionists.

The communities describing themselves as Reformed churches or 'those of the Reformed religion' were by the end of our period mainly located in Switzerland and Geneva (not strictly Swiss), south-west Germany, France, the Low Countries, England, and Scotland, with smaller pockets in Ireland and Eastern Europe. This tradition, characterized by considerable pluralism, developed out of the teachings not only of Zwingli and Calvin but of others with less familiar names: Martin Bucer (1491–1551), Heinrich Bullinger (1504–75), Peter Martyr Vermigli (1500–62) and many others. The term 'Calvinism' is often used for the tradition as a whole, but should be applied to the 16th century only with great caution. 'Calvinist' was essentially a term of abuse, never accepted by the Reformed, except in a most qualified way. We need to remember how diverse and broadly based the Reformed were, not to reduce them to a single brand of 'Calvinism', whether derived from Calvin or his immediate followers.

How did the post-Reformation Church of England fit into the map of mainstream Protestantism? Religion in Henry VIII's reign after his break with Rome has been helpfully, if crudely, described as 'Catholicism without the pope', although the regime did swing spasmodically between humanist-style attacks on traditional piety and traditionalist formulations of doctrine. However, by the end of Edward VI's reign and after the 'settlement of religion' under Elizabeth I, the doctrinal identity of the clerical and lay élites in the Church of England became predominantly Reformed. In the past it was often argued that the English church's doctrinal moderation distinguished it from other Protestant churches: that it was a *via media* between the Roman Catholic Church and the extremes of Continental Protestantism. This has had the unfortunate effect of reinforcing the notion that the Church of England embodied a distinctively English tradition, independent of intellectual developments on the Continent. The Church of England after the Elizabethan Settlement saw itself as one of the Reformed churches, but this did not entail any subservience to Calvin's Geneva. Although the 'godly' or 'Puritan' elements who perceived the Church of England as 'but half-reformed' did want it reshaped after foreign templates, especially that of Geneva, those described as 'conformists', committed both to the Church of England's sisterhood with the rest of the Reformed and to upholding the established form of religion, could and did argue, with increasing confidence by the end of the century, that the Church of England was rather the best of the Reformed churches, an exemplar for others.

In the middle decades of the 16th century the theological boundaries between Lutheran and Reformed gradually hardened. The period after the mid-1560s is often called the 'era of orthodoxy' in mainstream Protestantism. Not only Protestant, but also post-Tridentine Catholic, theologians concentrated on careful elaboration of their own 'purified' traditions as well as vitriolic polemic against opponents. Yet, despite all the retrenchment and rigid demarcation, this was a time of theological cross-fertilization: Lutherans and Reformed were avid readers of the end-of-century disputes between Jesuits and Dominicans on grace, freewill, and predestination, and even happily borrowed elements to use in their own intra-Protestant disputes.

Medieval scholasticism, with its precise definitions and careful distinctions, had been criticized by reformers of all hues for its distance from the religion of ordinary people, but it is arguable that the 'new' high theologies produced by the Reformations did not narrow that chasm. Few outside the educated clergy and laity could have grasped the complex issues dividing Christians. But if the masses had only a limited grasp of doctrinal nuances, church authorities were much more adept than their medieval forebears at enforcing formal orthodoxy and rooting out deviance. By the end of the century, Protestant and Catholic traditions had become set around groupings of simple formulas, symbols, and rituals. Although their piety was more streamlined than in the past, and scrutinized with greater zeal by ecclesiastical authority, ordinary Roman Catholics continued to concentrate on what had been central to late-medieval Catholics: the mystery of the mass with its re-enactment of Calvary and the conversion of the host into 'the body of Christ'; devotion to the Mother of God and the saints with their efficacious images and relics; prayer for departed relatives, friends, and benefactors; the forgiveness of sins in baptism, and the sacrament of penance. Ordinary Lutherans came to define their religious identity through the crucifix, the singing of chorales, the presence of Christ in 'the sacrament of the altar', and the exorcism in baptism. Ordinary Reformed on the Continent and in Scotland developed attachments to metrical psalms, plain churches cleansed of idolatry, and long sermons. The 'godly' in the Church of England yearned for larger doses of these Reformed elements. The Edwardine Books of Common Prayer had been largely compiled by a theologian who eventually aligned himself with the Reformed, Thomas Cranmer. Though by their penchant for wordy exhortations, their spare ritual, and general theological content the 1552 and 1559 Prayer Books were definitely Reformed in ethos, they retained more traditional elements than was usual among the Reformed: a fixed structure of worship, little or no room for extempore prayers, an elaborate ecclesiastical calendar, compulsory use of a medieval vestment, the surplice, and signing with the cross in baptism. These and many other matters caused immense irritation to Puritans, but many conservative laity and eventually even theologians, otherwise impeccably Reformed in doctrine, became increasingly attached to them.

By the end of the century great diversity still existed in the Reformed and Lutheran traditions, but what of post-Tridentine Catholicism? We have seen that diversity still existed among Catholic theologians on important doctrines, but the general impression is of a uniformity unheard of in medieval Catholicism. The moderate Hussites, known as Utraquists or Calixtines, had had a chequered history of grudging toleration or persecution; in the 16th century Rome successfully suppressed their privilege of administering the chalice to the laity. In the face of the Protestant challenge, Rome was unwilling to compromise on this issue, or clerical celibacy, or vernacular liturgy, despite periodic pressure from the Holy Roman Empire for concessions, and the advocacy of compromise by such important figures as Cajetan. However, despite the missal of Pius V (1570), some vestiges of diversity (in liturgy at least) remained, for example, in the Ambrosian rite in Milan, defended by its great reforming archbishop, Charles Borromeo (1538–84). The severest challenge for claims to complete uniformity in post-Tridentine Catholicism came from eastern Catholic churches whose theological and liturgical heritages had received some protection from the decrees of the Council of Florence. At the end of the century Rome reaffirmed the legitimacy of a degree of pluralism in liturgy and canon law, if not doctrine, in its approval of the union with the Holy See of Byzantine rite Ukrainians in the 1595–6 Union of Brest-Litovsk, and of the East Syrian rite Malabar Christians of St Thomas at the Synod of Diamper (1599). It was not until the 17th century that the Eastern Orthodox (who rejected communion with the see of Rome) were forced to respond definitively to the warring camps of Latin Christianity. The richness and energy of the theologies produced by western Christianity in this period are undeniable, but it is arguable that the great tragedy of the 16th-century Reformations is that, however fecund they were with ideas, insights, and zeal, they also produced chasms of doctrine and practice wider than any previous schism in the Christian community, wider than that between Rome and Constantinople, more unbridgeable even than the divisions that arose from the ancient christological controversies. The mutual recognition of 'one faith, one baptism, one Lord of all' (Eph. 4: 5) and the achievement of a consensus on the legitimate bounds of diversity in the 'One, Holy, Catholic and Apostolic Church' remain, at the beginning of the 21st century, far-off goals.

Bradshaw, Brendan, and Duffy, Eamon (eds.), *Humanism, Reform and the Reformation: The Career of John Fisher* (1989).

Cameron, Euan, *The European Reformation* (1991).

Donnelly, J. P., 'Calvinist Thomism', *Viator*, 7 (1976), 441–55.

Duffy, Eamon, *The Stripping of the Altars: Traditional Religion in England 1400– 1580* (1992).

Gerrish, Brian, *Grace and Gratitude: The Eucharistic Theology of Calvin* (1993).

Hillerbrand, H. J. (ed. in chief), *Oxford Encyclopedia of the Reformation* (4 vols.; 1996).

Jones, Martin D. W., *The Counter-Reformation* (1995).

Kirk, James (ed.), *Humanism and Reform: The Church in Europe, England and Scotland, 1400–1643* (1991).

Küng, Hans, *Justification*, ET (1965).

Lane, A. N. S., 'Scripture, Tradition and Church: An Historical Survey', *Vox Evangelica*, 9 (1975), 37–55.

—— 'Calvin's Use of the Fathers and the Medievals', *Calvin Theological Journal*, 16 (1981), 149–205.

Leith, John H., *Creeds of the Churches*, rev. edn. (1973).

MacCulloch, Diarmaid, *The Later Reformation in England 1547–1603* (1990).

McGrath, Alister, *Reformation Thought: An Introduction*, 2nd edn. (1993).

McSorley, H. J., *Luther Right or Wrong?* (1968).

Muller, Richard, *Christ and the Decree: Christology and Predestination in Reformed Theology from Calvin to Perkins* (1986).

Oberman, Heiko, *The Harvest of Late Medieval Theology: Gabriel Biel and Late Medieval Nominalism* (1963).

Pelikan, Jaroslav, *Reformation of Church and Dogma (1300–1700)* (1989).

Raitt, Jill, *The Eucharistic Theology of Theodore Beza: Development of the Reformed Doctrine* (1972).

Tierney, Brian, *Foundations of the Conciliar Theory*, repr. (1968).

Wicks, Jared, *Cajetan Responds: A Reader in Reformation Controversy* (1978).

X

AUTHORITY AND REASON
The 17th century

※ + ※

Anthony Milton

FOR WESTERN CHRISTENDOM, THE CENTURY FOLLOWING
the Reformation was more than anything else the century of confessional dogmatics. The separated churches—
Roman Catholic, Lutheran, and Reformed—drew up
their own doctrinal systems, or confessions, and combined this
mental consolidation with an organizational one in which the
different churches became stable denominations with their
own constitutions and lifestyles which they sought to standardize
throughout their membership. The confessions—the Decrees
and Canons of the Council of Trent, the Lutheran Formula of
Concord, and among the Reformed the Belgic, Gallic, and
Helvetic Confessions, the Thirty-Nine Articles, and the Canons
of Dort—now stood as basic yardsticks of doctrinal orthodoxy,
against which people's writings and behaviour across a whole
range of Christian activities could be scrutinized and (if
necessary) condemned. Often born out of immediate problems
and struggles, these confessions rapidly became polemically defined credal statements, inflexible to any change. Attempts to
adjust or redraft them simply generated more hostility, as the
Dutch Arminians found when they sought to modify the Belgic
Confession, and with minor exceptions no new doctrinal statements with genuine 'confessional' status were drawn up after the
early years of the century. The authority of the confessions made
compromise or reconciliation between the different confessional

groupings all but impossible. It is hardly surprising, in these circumstances, that the century did not give rise to the original genius of a Luther or Calvin.

Superficially, the overall picture may thus seem to be one of a loss of vitality and creativity. After the glittering cavalry charges of the Reformation period, religious thinkers would appear to have settled down behind their heavily fortified trenches for a war of theological attrition. In contrast to the freedom and questioning of the earlier period, the 17th century can appear to have retreated into a stale and limited process of endless elaboration and conservative protection (in increasingly ossified forms) of the theological advances of the previous century. But this would be unfair. In fact, for a supposedly arid and conservative forum of religious debate, controversial divinity in this period was an area of constant flux and development. Some of the major alterations and most challenging new developments in Christian thought stem from the confessionally driven controversial divinity of the time, and are inseparable from it.

To begin with, confessionalism proved unable to close down debates within the different communions. On the contrary, a great deal of intellectual energy was devoted to internal conflicts and disputes within the individual confessions and churches. The Catholic Church was troubled by the *De Auxiliis* controversy between Jesuits and Dominicans and the Jansenist controversy; the Lutherans by the kenotic and syncretist controversies; the Dutch Reformed churches by the Arminian conflict and the Voetian/ Cocceian controversy; the French Reformed by the Amyraldian controversy; while the Church of England was rocked by a seemingly endless series of polemical debates over Arminianism and forms of church government and ceremonies, with a brief wholesale revision of its articles of faith in mid-century. Many of these controversies were concerned in one way or another with the dialectic of grace and free will, and the eternal problem of balancing God's sovereignty with human agency. For all the implacability of the confessional statements, change and division on this topic continued incessantly in the 17th century. This was partly because, even with a confessional constant, theological formulations change. Confessionalization was just one part of the systematization of earlier writers, and this required theologians to grapple with issues and doctrines which sixteenth-century authors had not dealt with in any detail. This systematization was accomplished by the increasing use of medieval methods of discourse, disputation, and philosophy. But this revival of scholasticism did not necessarily impose a dead weight of obscurantism on religious enquiry, but was itself a force for change. The increasing use of scholastic method forced an inevitable elaboration of doctrine which was in its way more searching than the less systematic assertions of the early Reformers. An elaboration of doctrine—especially concerning theological prolegomena and the essence and attributes of God—necessarily brought with it more interest in metaphysical problems, and the search for a more speculative, philosophically adequate language of theology.

Moreover, the confessions were not quite the inflexible monuments that they might appear. The Council of Trent's doctrinal position was notoriously subtle and ambiguous: it was, as contemporaries called it, a 'nose of wax' on many theological points, phrased in order to head off deep divisions among Roman Catholics themselves. But its very flexibility ensured that it could be read in many different ways, and the theological debates and divisions on the Roman side continued. In the Reformed communion, the idea of confessional community was compromised by a considerable degree of variance between the different confessions, yet at the same time there was much that could potentially be harmonized, thereby making appeal across the confessions possible for the different groups in dispute. When Reformed theologians gathered together at the Synod of Dort (1618–19), they discovered among themselves a rich diversity of views on questions surrounding the doctrine of grace but, despite a good deal of acrimony, they were able to generate sufficient compromises and qualifications to produce an agreed set of doctrinal formulations against Arminianism. The conviction of a shared confessional identity could in these cases often be more vital than doctrinal unanimity in keeping the confessions to-gether.

The continuing controversies between the different confessions were also not the stale, unproductive exercise that they might appear. To begin with, the confessional boundaries erected by polemicists did not necessarily correspond to theological reality. Christians constantly borrowed from different theological traditions, even if they remained formally at variance and on one or two topics always expressed themselves in terms of violent opposition. Participants in the Arminian or *De Auxiliis* controversies could often find their positions closer to those of their confessional rivals than those of their ostensible confessional partners—Dominican authors and Jansenist divines, for example, were regularly cited by Calvinist theologians in support of their more severely Augustinian doctrine, against the arguments of Arminian writers.

Moreover, the erection of tightly bound, scholastic theological systems in defence of established confessions did not produce a simple stalemate, or close down creative theological debate. It is true that there may have been little meaningful dialogue between the confessions, and that they continued to clash over the familiar issues of merit, justification, eucharistic doctrine, papal authority, ubiquitarianism, idolatry, free will, antinomianism, and so on. The acceptance of the permanent separation of the confessional groupings did nothing to lessen the energy which they devoted to seeking to undermine each other's positions. Nevertheless, this polemical determination meant that the basic assumptions behind the different confessions were subjected to the most searching and damaging scrutiny, so that the very basis of religious knowledge and certainty was called into question.

New scholarly fronts were opened up. Clashes over the different confessions' claims to catholicity, for example, generated a remarkable surge of interest in patristics and church history, among Protestants as much as Catholics. All confessional groupings claimed to be 'catholic' in the sense of preserving the tradition of the fathers. The views of the church fathers thus became one of the battlegrounds of religious polemic, but in the process patristic scholarship made great strides forward. The first-ever critical patrology was written by the great Lutheran scholar Johann Gerhard (1582–1637), who coined the term. The degree of Protestant enthusiasm for the church fathers did differ, however. Where Georg Calixtus (1586–1656) and the other Lutheran Syncretists taught that the consensus of the first five centuries of church fathers could provide a secondary source of doctrine to supplement scripture, most Lutherans were less convinced, and Gerhard's patrology itself sought more systematically to provide a guide to where the fathers were to be followed and where they had 'erred'. The problem for Protestants in particular was that, as post-Tridentine patristic scholarship became more systematic (exemplified in the voluminous *Annales Ecclesiastici* of Cesare Baronius (1538–1607), but also in many other editions of patristic texts), so it became increasingly difficult to make the fathers fit into later doctrinal divisions. The Huguenot theologian Isaac Casaubon (1559–1614) was deeply troubled when he found himself unable to find patristic support for the French Reformed doctrine of the Eucharist. Another Huguenot theologian, Jean Daillé (1594–1670), sought a more radical solution to this problem when he emphasized the inconsistency of patristic testimony in his *Traicté de l'employ des saincts pères* (1631).

Daillé's work was to be very influential in the long run, but did not secure unanimous Protestant support. In the Church of England a strong emphasis on the importance of the early church fathers as a secondary source both of doctrine and ecclesiology led to attempts by Lancelot Andrewes, William Laud, and other churchmen to adjust aspects of the liturgy and doctrine of the church accordingly. Among Laud's followers were two of Daillé's most prominent Protestant opponents—Henry Hammond (1605–60) and John Pearson (1613–86) (who effectively refuted Daillé's attacks on the reliability of the Ignatian epistles)—although later Anglicans (like other Reformed divines) were strongly influenced by the French theologian.

Daillé's *Traicté* was itself in part a contribution to another increasingly problematic aspect of the Catholic/Protestant debate, and that was concerned with the long-running argument over the 'rule of faith'. Protestants challenged the Catholic claim to apostolic tradition and papal authority as the criterion for distinguishing true from false faith. In response, Catholics attacked the Protestant claim to scripture as the sole criterion of faith by challenging the notion that scripture was self-authenticating, or that inner persuasion could assure the reader of the truth of the scriptures, and that human reason could serve as the proper mechanism for scriptural interpretation. Protestants did not simply appeal to enlightened reason for the interpretation of scripture, and even when it came to the initial conviction that the scriptures were indeed true, not all Protestants simply claimed the importance of inner persuasion. In England, for example, the Caroline Divines still urged the importance of the church in initially drawing people to the scriptures, and the growing tendency of Church of England divines to emphasize the importance of the physical continuity of the church's witness led their clash with Roman Catholic apologists to concentrate particularly on the succession of the true church via the oft-repeated Catholic demand, 'Where was your church before Luther?'

The debate took an especially critical turn in France, where Catholic controversialists such as François Veron sought to strengthen their assault on Protestantism by turning to forms of 'Pyrrhonism'—a form of undogmatic scepticism that proposed to suspend judgement on a wide range of questions, including whether or not something could be known. In the process, they attacked the very notion that rational faculties could serve as the foundation and support of the faith, seeking to show that Protestants could have no assured faith once they had rejected the church as an infallible judge. This Catholic attack reached its climax in the work of Richard Simon (1638–1712) who endeavoured in his *Critical History of the Old Testament* (1678) to demonstrate that scripture was not self-authenticating, and denied the Mosaic authorship of the Pentateuch. While Simon sought to use all his scholarship as a club against the Calvinists who claimed religious truth from the bible alone, he was in the process adopting many of the techniques of biblical criticism of Baruch Spinoza (1632–77), who had developed them with a very different intent. Spinoza pushed matters further by insisting on the separation of theology and philosophy, leaving the role of theology as simply that of teaching piety, obedience, and a moral life. René Descartes's principle of 'universal doubt' and insistence on a universal method had similarly questioned by implication the immunity of theology and biblical scholarship from the dictates of natural philosophy. While some elements of such ideas could be used to attack Protestantism, they harboured more fundamental dangers for the basis of all Christian confessions.

The intention of the Roman Catholic Pyrrhonists was to undermine belief in self-authenticating scripture, in order to place the greatest importance on the witness of the Catholic Church. The Protestant response to this challenge could vary, throwing its emphasis variously on scripture, reason, or inner persuasion as offering the key to religious certainty. Lutherans in the later 17th century redoubled their emphasis on the truthfulness of scripture. A more commonly embraced solution, however, for those who took on board some of the assaults on scripture and the fathers, was the championing of a form of mitigated scepticism, which granted the impossibility of infallible certainty but sought instead to elevate human reason as the only means of assessing degrees of probability, in contrast to the scriptural absolutism or patristic confidence of earlier writers. This became especially prominent in Anglican thought in the later 17th century, in the writings of the 'Latitudinarians', including theologians such as John Wilkins (1614–72) who sought to bridge the gap between theological method and the 'new philosophy' by the use of reason.

An alternative approach to the importance of reason emerged in the thought of the Cambridge Platonists. Scholars like Benjamin Whichcote (1609–83) and Henry More (1614–87) attached vital importance in the development of religious knowledge to 'reason', not in the Latitudinarian sense of a natural, impersonal human capacity, but rather in mystical terms as 'the candle of the Lord', a means whereby the individual human soul gained illumination by participation in the divine reason. This equation of human with divine reason, and emphasis on the experiential witness of divine inspiration, offered another response to the 'rule of faith' debate. Here too, the Cambridge Platonists had obvious affinities with the many evangelical groups throughout the century who emphasized the importance of inner experience as a primary authority in religious life, with an increasing stress on the doctrine of the Holy Spirit, and a readiness to identify the spirit in scripture with God's Spirit in the individual. It was the Quakers who moved one crucial step further by their dissociation of the Word and Spirit, and their insistence that, where there was a discrepancy, the Word should be tried by the Spirit rather than vice versa. There was an enormous difference between the rational Logos theory of the Cambridge Platonists and the theology of the Holy Spirit that humble Quakers worked out from their own religious experience. But both groups, along with the wide range of other pietistic groups active in the period, were expressive of the crisis of religious authority that the Reformation had unleashed, and that showed no sign of abating in the 17th century.

The involved relationship of scripture to experience and inward revelation was also reflected in the extraordinary flowering of mystical and apocalyptic prophecy and eschatology in the 17th century. This was the age, not just of confessional dogmatists, but of the German shoemaker-mystic Jacob Boehme (1575–1624), of the extraordinary Rosicrucian manifestos which created such excitement throughout Europe, and of Thomas Venner's attempt in 1661 to overthrow the government of England in order to erect the Fifth Monarchy, as foretold in Daniel. Nevertheless, a vivid eschatology and prophetical excitement were not simply the preserve of sectarian fanatics, but built on established foundations. Some forces of mystical prophecy and apocalyptic inquiry and prediction were evident in the confessional churches themselves,

though in sometimes tense relationship with confessional orthodoxy. In Germany in the late 16th and early 17th centuries prophetic enquiry in both the Lutheran and Calvinist confessions was
remarkably intense. Boehme's bizarre fusion of Gnostic, Christian
Platonist, and Paracelsian ideas and influences was *sui generis*, but
other writers such as Jacob Arndt (1555–1621) were more mainstream thinkers whose prediction of the imminent end of the
world inspired even scholars such as Johann Gerhard. German
Calvinism and Lutheranism were alike homes to increasingly
eclectic forms of mystical and chiliastic thinking, where eschatological prophecy was combined with astrology, hermeticism, al-
chemy, and cabbalistic ideas. Moreover, while Boehme's cosmic
vision rejected apocalyptic prophecy and was opposed to historical and literal chiliasm, other groups were more ready to tie
prophecies directly to current events and the confessional warfare that was devastating the country.

One particularly potent idea to emerge from this brew of
mystical and utopian ideas was a new millennialism. A number
of thinkers—most prominently Johann Heinrich Alsted in Calvinist Herborn, and in England Joseph Mede (1586–1638), who had
been troubled by Pyrrhonistic inclinations in his youth, broke
with past apocalyptic interpretation in reserving the prophesied
thousand-year rule of the saints for a future millennial reign on
earth, rather than placing it in the past with the binding of Satan
in the years between AD 300 and 1300. This millenarian doctrine,
combined with utopian ideas and heightened expectations, all
conveyed in popular tracts and speeches, equipped both mainstream but also more radical prophets with the intellectual gun-
powder necessary to fuel an eschatological drive for apocalyptic
reform of church, state, and society. Both Germany and England
experienced an explosion of apocalyptic writing at times of political crisis—the Thirty Years War and the English Civil War re-
spectively. In both cases earlier apocalyptic and mystical writings
were reprinted and applied far more directly to current events,
and in both countries such apocalyptic speculation became very
heavily politicized as a result. However, in both Germany and

England, a reaction against such prophecy set in later in the century. Both Lutheran and Reformed churches became increasingly concerned that key doctrines were being threatened by chiliastic ideas. Both in Lutheran Germany and in England, the politicization of prophecy seems to have been followed by its collapse. There may well be a causal relationship, here: perhaps not so much that increasingly specific prophecies were proved wrong, but that long wars and increasingly complex political crises seemed to defy beliefs that they were to be suddenly and swiftly resolved by divine intervention. In England, moreover, the association of apocalyptic prophecy with political revolution made it increasingly unpalatable. In both countries, apocalyptic prophecy became spiritualized, the emphasis being placed on Antichrist as a more general force of sin and evil, and the conviction that the kingdom of God was to be erected in the heart of the believer rather than in the national polity. A similar trajectory towards the internalization of reformation and renewal is visible across the Continent and its confessional boundaries, among English Puritans, French Jansenists, and German Lutherans.

This move towards the cultivation of inner piety is as prominent a theme in the Christian thought of the 17th century as the rise of confessionalism. Indeed, enthusiasts of such trends often saw themselves as representing the vital obverse to confessionalism, as upholders of true active faith opposing the stale, 'dead' faith of logic-chopping confessionalism, where dry academic debate had led people to forget and ignore true religion. This urgent desire for a renewal of Christian life is evident time and again throughout the century. What often appears as a vast cross-confessional wave engulfed Europe in the 17th century, with all countries and confessions witnessing the emergence of movements of ascetic mysticism, moral rigorism, and affective piety that championed a living faith in opposition to mere external show and words. In Catholicism, the writings of the bishop of Geneva, Francis de Sales (1567–1622), provided a programme for laypeople to pursue spiritual perfection. Several distinctive religious movements also emerged, most notably that of Jansenism—

which espoused a sternly Augustinian moral rigorism—and the quietists, who adopted a less Augustinian form of mystical meditation. The same period also saw a remarkable rise in devotion to the sacred heart of Jesus, which was given a careful theological explanation and justification by Jean Eudes (1601–80). Independently of such developments, in England, Puritan thinkers professed a profound concern for the inward religious life, developing intense forms of personal piety based around assurance of election. The tradition of Puritan spiritual narratives that developed out of such trends continued throughout the century, reaching its apogee in John Bunyan's *Pilgrim's Progress*. These forms of Puritan affective piety also manifested themselves in more extreme forms—in the preaching of Scottish and Irish revivalists, in the millenarian and enthusiastic sects of the 1640s and 1650s, and in radical Puritan movements which split apart from Reformed Protestantism altogether, in the shape of the Muggletonians, Quakers, and Antinomians. The Quakers perhaps constituted the logical end of a trend which had insisted on de-emphasizing the significance of all external observances, institutions, and forms in the face of the centrality of the direct individual experience of God. Similar movements emerged in German Pietism and the Dutch *nadere reformatie*, which in their different strands placed varying emphasis on the importance of mysticism, penance, and the role of the clergy in guiding Christians in the cultivation of true inward holiness.

It is easy to see the rationale of the growth of a stress on inward assurance as an answer to the questioning of the basis of religious knowledge by the epistemology of Descartes and others. But it would be wrong to lump these different streams together, or to depict them in simple opposition to an arid confessional mainstream. To begin with, while these different movements might have been united in their opposition to 'dead faith', they were often deeply divided over the question of how far they should separate from the outside world, and over the role of the Spirit in practical divinity. For example, in contrast to the German Pietists, the 'Dutch Pietists' emphasized practical divinity but were vigorously against mysticism, and were deeply preoccupied with the *political* aspects of religious renewal, calling for action in *every* sphere of life. Many English Puritans who were dedicated exponents of practical divinity were similarly determined to reform the government and organization of the church as part of their programme of religious renewal. The different groups also quarrelled violently with one another. Advocates of anxious self-scrutiny and moral rigorism were often the vigorous opponents of those who emphasized the immediate, liberating experience of grace. In this sense, the acrimonious antinomian controversy in Puritan New England found its echo in the hostilities between Jansenists and quietists, and in the almost universal condemnation of the Quakers. The intense vigour with which the different groups opposed each other suggests that they did not see themselves as a single movement, even if their polemic was sometimes motivated by a realization that their antagonists were embarrassingly close to some of their own convictions.

If anything united these different groups, it was their common rejection of formal, 'dead faith'. But the fact that it became fashionable for many to define their religious convictions against cold, dry, hair-splitting theology does not mean that there was also a body of theologians dedicated to 'formalist' emotionless theology. In fact, the latter was a form of theology that was only ever invoked as an 'other' for individuals to define themselves against. In reality, the foremost theological logicians often had a profound concern for spirituality as well, and their fervent desire to uphold the nostrums of orthodoxy sprang in part from a sincere conviction that they thereby protected religious truths that were crucial to the cultivation of a proper and active Christian faith. Many elements of the reaction against mere 'formal, dead faith' were axiomatic to those divines who were themselves at the forefront of confessional scholasticism. Some of the greatest systematic theologians of the century were also prominent devotional writers. The Catholic Cardinal Bellarmine (1542–1621), the Lutheran Johann Gerhard, and the English Puritan William Perkins (1558–1602) were all popular devotional writers whose scholasticism was combined with a deep concern with the practicalities of Christian life and practice. Two of the most prominent early Dutch Pietists, Gisbert Voetius (1589–1676) and William Ames (1576–1633), had been enthusiastic participants at the condemnation of Arminianism at the Synod of Dort. The predestinarian doctrines of later Calvinism were not arcane and dusty dogmatics, but had a strong christological foundation and a firm experiential emphasis.

Many of these movements for revival of interior piety emerged naturally out of trends visible within orthodox confessionalism, and it may be most helpful to see them partly as different manifestations of elements of tension and ambiguity within orthodox religion. In essence, the struggle between the 'religion of the heart' and confessional dogmas was not so much a struggle between different religious groups, but rather a conflict that was played out in the mind of every active Christian thinker. Early modern confessionalism created a situation where a hostile observer could easily protest that doctrinal formularies were being prized above Christian living: and it was this perception that generated the urgent demands for an anti-formalist religion, which in themselves created a still more anxious defence of confessional norms that might be violated in such a reaction. What does seem clear, however, is a gradual movement later in the 17th century in all these different pietistic traditions—in England, Germany, France, and the Netherlands—away from attempting to transform society and the church, and instead retreating from the world into the internal, experiential life, and often into separatist conventicles. A more general rejection of theocratic principles is increasingly evident.

Another development associated with the rise of Pietism, and a declining belief in the idea of a godly magistrate, is that of a full-blooded notion of religious toleration. This did not necessarily emerge from any of the ecumenical notions that occasionally found expression among the confessional churches. The reunification of the churches was a regular source of debate and discussion among religious writers of this period, and inspired the actions of committed ecumenists such as John Dury (1596–1680). Various attempts were made by adherents of confessional groups throughout the century to draw up agreed definitions of funda- mental articles of faith, and there were amicable discussions be- tween Calvinists and Lutherans at the Leipzig Colloquy (1631), but there was never any real likelihood that confessional barriers would be breached, and nothing was achieved. It was those writers who rejected the precepts of confessionalism—rationalist philosophers or enthusiastic sectaries—who developed the most inclusive views of religious society. But even when increasing numbers of writers were ready to maintain that the Christian magistrate had no right to punish heretics and schismatics, they usually drew the line somewhere. Even the radically inclusive Roger Williams (c.1604–83), in his *The Bloudy Tenent of Persecution* (1644) did not allow atheism and blasphemy. Nevertheless, in the writings of Williams and John Locke in England, and of Simon Episcopius (1583–1643) and other Remonstrant divines in the Netherlands, the notion that religious diversity was not merely something that might be reluctantly tolerated for political reasons, but might actually be a positive good, began to be regu- larly expressed, although it could not yet hope to find a positive reception from society.

The end of the 17th century, then, was marked in many coun- tries by a retreat from the incessant demands of political confessionalization, and of theocratic notions of government. This was a change that was at times combined with the develop- ment of new notions of scriptural interpretation and natural the- ology that challenged some of the presuppositions of confessionalism, and with the emergence of radically secularizing ideas of toleration and individualism, and of religious ideals that were quietist rather than political, and centred on voluntaristic associations rather than national churches. But these were not developments that carried all before them. It was the impracti- calities of confessionalization that more than anything served to subdue it, combined perhaps with a genuine revulsion for the religious upheavals and fanaticism that had characterized the

Thirty Years War and the English Civil War. But there was no sudden end to heresy-hunting, or to the general conviction that religious unity was politically desirable. The century ended, not just with the publications of John Locke, but also with the suppression of Socinianism in Poland, and the revocation of the Edict of Nantes in France. Religious censorship continued even in the notoriously liberal Dutch Republic. It would be a long time before the tide of confessionalism truly receded.

Barnes, Robin Bruce, *Prophecy and Gnosis: Apocalypticism in the Wake of the Lutheran Reformation* (1988).

Beeke, Joel R., *Assurance of Faith: Calvin, English Puritanism and the Dutch Second Reformation* (1991).

Campbell, T., *The Religion of the Heart: A Study of European Religious Life in the Seventeenth and Eighteenth Centuries* (1991).

Firth, Katherine R., *The Apocalyptic Tradition in Reformation Britain, 1530–1645* (1979).

Grell, O. P., and Scribner, R. (eds.), *Tolerance and Intolerance in the European Reformation* (1996).

Muller, Richard H., *Post-Reformation Reformed Dogmatics*, i. *Prolegomena* (1987).

Nuttall, Geoffrey, *The Holy Spirit in Puritan Faith and Experience* (1946).

Pelikan, Jaroslav, *The Christian Tradition: A History of the Development of Doctrine*, iv. *Reformation of Church and Dogma (1400–1700)* (1984).

Popkin, Richard H., *The History of Scepticism from Erasmus to Spinoza* (1979).

Preus, R. D., *The Theology of Post-Reformation Lutheranism* (2 vols.; 1970).

Yates, Frances, *The Rosicrucian Enlightenment* (1972).

XI

CERTAINTY AND TOLERANCE
The 18th century

John Kent

T HE 'LONG 18TH CENTURY', WHICH STRETCHES FROM the 1660s to as late as the 1830s, from the impact of the ideas of Locke and Newton on European society in the later seventeenth century to the time when Europe was slowly assimilating the consequences of the French Revolution, is a historian's convention, but it is relevant to the history of western Christianity because these were the years in which the Christian churches first found their social and intellectual position in European society threatened by the critical assaults of an aggressive modernity. The medieval western church had divided into Protestant and Roman Catholic institutions in the 16th century; in the 18th, as the importance of that break-up declined, organized Christianity faced new sources of conflict. In this context the 18th-century Enlightenment was above all a series of challenges to long-accepted authorities, religious, scientific, and philosophical: changing ideas, especially in the fields of physics and historical studies, deeply affected the churches as well as society as a whole. There was no simple black-and-white conflict, but a long drawn-out sifting of traditional certainties.

From this point of view the 18th century may easily seem to have been disastrous for the Christian churches. The French historian, Delumeau, thought that by the end of the 18th century the running-down of successive Protestant and Catholic campaigns to convert the ordinary people of Europe to Christianity, which had been going on ever since the Reformation, had become clear; and Vovelle has written of the 18th century as a time of 'dechristianization', at any rate in France. This was not the whole of the story, however. In the case of Christian worship, for example, Protestant church music was transformed by Johann Sebastian Bach and Georg Friedric Handel, while congregational singing entered a new era through the hymns of Isaac Watts and the Wesley brothers. Between the late 17th and the mid-18th century there was a tremendous outbreak of Protestant revival preaching, not dissimilar, on the practical level, to the older Jesuit methods of mission-preaching, though the theologies involved differed. This was the basis of what is usually called the Evangelical Revival, through which Protestantism, which had seemed in danger of falling to pieces in the later 17th century, regrouped, and rapidly acquired a new and vitally important power-base in North America. This revivified popular Protestantism, in both its German and British forms, firmly retained a belief in the authority of the Christian scriptures as a final divine self-revelation. Both John Wesley and his fellow-Anglican, the philosophical theologian Joseph Butler, sought in different ways to assert the absoluteness of a Christian understanding of creation in which the human race depended for its ultimate happiness on salvation from sin through Christ. And European Catholicism not only survived the fiery tests of the 1790s, but successfully relaunched itself in the following century.

Nevertheless, the Enlightenment bulks large in any account of the religious history of the period. The Enlightenment is often described as a radically anti-Christian, though not necessarily anti-religious, movement among a relatively small number of 18th-century intellectuals, who are said to have shared an over-optimistic belief in the capacity of human society, guided by reason, science, and education, to make progress towards perfection. Among the 18th-century thinkers typical of the Enlightenment looked at as a movement for intellectual freedom were such French intellectuals as Denis Diderot, editor with d'Alembert of the subtly anti-Roman Catholic *Encyclopédie*; Jean-Jacques

Rousseau, who invented his own civic religion, the purpose of which was to give moral stability to the ideal political community of his *Social Contract* (1762); and Voltaire, a pessimistic theist, who thought that society needed to be saved from the Christian churches. The greatest figure of the German Enlightenment, Gotthold Lessing, attacked Christianity as intellectually intolerant and was himself inclined to pantheism, in the style of the Jewish philosopher, Baruch Spinoza. The work of these men was characteristic of what in the course of the 18th century became a self-conscious intellectual movement, whose leaders saw themselves as possessing a liberated, hopeful, non-Christian, and, in the case of some of them, atheistic understanding of the present position and future possibilities of humanity. But this was not a revolutionary political movement: there was no direct link between such writers and the Jacobins of the French Revolution. For the handful of people most passionately involved no political revolution was necessary: they thought in terms of reason's gradual, irresistible advance towards greater and greater clarity. They identified Christianity with darkness and superstition: Edward Gibbon, the English historian, for example, described the thousand years between the end of the Roman empire in the west and the fall of Constantinople in 1453 as the triumph of barbarism and religion.

The Enlightenment, however, was not simply an affair of intellectuals which broke out suddenly as the *ancien régime* entered the 'enlightened despot' stage of its struggles to modernize. What also caused many 18th-century people to think of theirs as an enlightened age was a broad pattern of social and intellectual changes which had been going on in Europe and also in the Americas between the 16th century and the French Revolution of 1789, and which modified the way in which many ordinary educated people thought about human nature and religion. One of the more remarkable examples of how the general view of the supernatural was altering by the end of the 17th century in much of Europe and North America was the quite sudden shift of opinion against holding witchcraft trials, and against the consequent execution of both men and women on the ground that they were witches. However one explains the great witch-panics, the Christian churches had largely accepted this magical world-view as part of their theological environment. There had been no real doubt about the existence of demonic forces, and both theologians and ecclesiastical authorities had been involved in the trials of alleged witches. Nevertheless, both trials and executions became socially unacceptable by the end of the 18th century. This does not mean that there was an overall decrease in the amount of human cruelty: the Jacobins executed people wholesale on political grounds, and this has been seen as an indirect outcome of the Enlightenment.

The disappearance from most of Europe of witchcraft as a serious social and religious problem went with a shrinking of the hold on the imagination of the more educated classes of the Christian doctrine of providence, which is concerned with the divine government of the creation. What many people began to doubt was the possibility of supernatural intervention in nature, thought of as the world of physical experience, and witchcraft offered a crude example of alleged supernatural activity. There is no agreed explanation of how the change came about, though it is clear that those who administered justice became less and less confident about the nature and quality of the 'confessions' that were put before them, and about the use of torture in the legal system to extort them. From a practical point of view the protest against judicial torture was summed up by a leading figure of the Italian Enlightenment, Cesare Beccaria, in his book, *On Crime and Punishment* (1764), and the roots of Amnesty International are to be found in the enlightened view of the rights of the individual over against all forms of social and political power. In Tuscany, Beccaria's influence led to the abolition of the death penalty, a unique action in the 18th century. Modern, by no means universally successful, protests against capital punishment have depended heavily on the typically 'enlightened' fear of error, of executing an individual who should not have been executed. In England, the 16th-century law that sanctioned prosecution for alleged witchcraft was repealed in 1736; the last European execution of someone charged with witchcraft may have been in Poland in 1793. At much the same time it was becoming socially impossible to execute people on the ground that they were heretics or blasphemers, though imprisonment remained a possibility in many countries.

The move toward greater reliance on human reason was as much a social product as the by-product of philosophical argument. One direct source of increased 'enlightenment' was the steady accumulation of fresh evidence about human life and its environment. This evidence often clashed with what had been transmitted by tradition, or asserted on the basis of a combination of scriptural statements and classical philosophical categories. The relationship between classical antiquity and the European present changed steadily between 1600 and 1800. It became absurd to suggest, as John Wesley, for example, still did in the later 18th century, that 'modern' music, by which he meant the music of Bach and Handel, had much less power over the human soul than the music of the Greeks; but when J. W. Goethe visited Assisi in 1786 he deliberately ignored the Franciscan basilica and went instead to look at the surviving portico of the Roman temple which was now used as a Catholic church. Geographical and astronomical discovery, Newtonian physics, and Harvey's demonstration of the circulation of the blood were among changes of scientific perception which led a broad section of the educated élites of Europe and America to modify their world-view. They accepted the essential accuracy of the new information, and they were not easily tempted into a theological assessment of their widening knowledge. They were therefore gradually ceasing to treat either the bible or the Christian churches as the major source of their understanding of the physical universe, the planet itself, or the history of the diverse human races inhabiting it. When Diderot, for example, poured scorn on the assumption that because a French naval expedition in the 1770s had set foot on Tahiti the French were entitled to annex the island and enslave its inhabitants, he made it clear that he did not think that the French could plead a superiority in religion as part of their justification. The Tahitians were entitled to their own world-view.

Behind these changes of attitude lay a shift in the European world-view, the growth of the belief that the individual human being did not, in order to think and act correctly, have to submit to external, traditional authority, even when authority came in the written form of alleged divine self-revelation, as in the case of the Jewish and Christian scriptures, or to the religious institutions established on the basis of such an authority. As early as 1678 the Catholic scholar, Richard Simon, in his *Histoire critique du Vieux Testament*, was seeking to establish the right of biblical criticism, as it was later called, to question the limits set by ecclesiastical authority to free discussion. Simon himself was anathematized by the church, but his book was still read. In the long run the 'enlightened' scholar insisted on the freedom to construct his/ her own version of the text and of its 'original' meaning. In the 19th century Liberal Protestantism continued the 'enlightened' approach, as did Catholic modernism at the beginning of the 20th century. As in Simon's case, both groups of scholars met considerable ecclesiastical resistance.

This more critical attitude to the bible was symptomatic of the way in which the European cultural situation had been changing since the 16th century. There was a decrease in the number of people who assumed that the Christian 'revelation' could be used to provide final definitions of human nature, its purpose, and its fate. The philosophical theology of the great figures of 17th-century philosophy, René Descartes, Thomas Hobbes, and John Locke, already related much more to human reason than to divine revelation. These 'enlightened' tendencies were expressed with extreme boldness between 1690 and 1730 in the writings of the English deists, a small group of intellectuals, among them Anthony Collins, whose best-known book was entitled, significantly, *A Discourse of Freethinking* (1713), Samuel Clarke, and John Toland, who published *Christianity not Mysterious* in 1696. They were deeply alienated from traditional Christianity, and, although they have often been underrated, they should be included in the general picture of the British Enlightenment. They thought that the individual's own reason, whether thought of as God-given, or as somehow the natural product of a basic substance or matter, should be his fundamental guide, and reason was understood as primarily a free, critical instrument, depending on knowledge, logic, and judgement for its results. Among these results might be the knowledge of God and of the moral behaviour which he required, though Collins was probably an atheist and Toland became a pantheist. There was no need for a specifically Christian revelation; there was talk of 'natural religion' and of a 'moral sense'. As for the Anglican George Berkeley, his brilliantly obscure anti-materialist apologetic had no effect on his contemporaries in the great wave of enthusiasm for Newtonian science.

Eighteenth-century Britain offers an example of 'enlightenment' as a kind of 'conservative modernism' (J. G. A. Pocock). There was no tremendous tension, but freedom of thought, freedom of religious belief, freedom of publication, freedom of political action, all quietly increased and became part of an attitude which looked back to an idealized classical city-state more than it looked forward to modern experiments in mass democracy. Religion was valued if it helped to stabilize society. The cautious, ironical, sceptical philosopher, David Hume, extended the normal Protestant rejection of alleged latter-day miracles back into the NT, but he made no direct challenge to the Anglican apologist, Joseph Butler, who had argued that the first converts became Christians in terms of miracles, and that their testimony was the same kind of evidence as if they had put it in writing and these writings had survived (*The Analogy of Religion* (1736), 257).

A major consequence of the Enlightenment was a widening gap between 'popular' and 'official' Christianity. In the case of the Protestant churches the cultural effects of the Reformation directly contributed to the spread of what came to be called 'enlightened' attitudes. In some parts of the 18th-century Catholic Church there was a distinct reaction against Counter-Reformation piety. In Italy, for example, L. A. Muratori, one of the founders of the modern (enlightened) approach to historical scholarship, criticized popular enthusiasm for a definition of the doctrine of the Assumption of the Virgin Mary, and was answered by

Alphonsus Liguori in *The Glories of Mary* (1750). The Habsburg emperor, Joseph II, who ruled between 1765 and 1790, tried to reduce what he regarded as superstition among the less educated of his subjects. At the popular level, therefore, belief in Christianity as a source of supernatural intervention in ordinary life had to find new means of expression, and from this point of view Protestant evangelical revivalism, which in its early creative phase was a search for supernatural power, and which rejoiced in what were regarded as 'special providences' of God on the individual's behalf, has to be interpreted as 'counter-Enlightenment'.

Yet another major element in this gradual transformation of attitudes in Europe and the Americas was that by the end of the 17th century the struggle between the Roman Catholic and the Protestant Churches had reached a point at which it became clear that Protestantism would survive the long Catholic counter-offensive. Both parties continued to affirm that theirs was the pure form of primitive Christianity, but the educated élites of Europe ceased to think of the choice as a major intellectual issue. There were still many people who, for various reasons, accepted the view that the state had the right to choose and impose a particular version of Christianity on its subjects, but the approach was breaking down in favour of some concept of religious toleration. The most sustained example of the traditional policy was the relentless anti-Protestant drive of the ageing Louis XIV, determined (and failing) to make France a totally Roman Catholic country, but it was the subtle arguments in favour of an absolute toleration of religious deviance by a French Protestant exile in Holland, Pierre Bayle, which pointed to the future. The demand for freedom of thought and publication, though often challenged since the 18th century on the grounds that public welfare cannot indefinitely tolerate the extremes of free human expression on such themes as racism or religious belief, was a vital element in the Enlightenment's legacy. There was a shift of power as 'public opinion', which in the 18th century meant 'enlightened opinion', became an independent force demanding official acceptance as a legitimate part of cultural and political processes. Society increasingly rejected constraint by religious institutions and presuppositions, as well as by the arbitrary will of government. From this point of view, it is difficult to argue that modern western culture draws its vitality principally from the Christian tradition.

In the history of the Enlightenment's influence on 18th-century religion the American Revolution (1776) is more important than the French (1789). At the heart of the American rebellion lay a determination to break with the authority of both the Church of England and the Hanoverian dynasty. The American leaders happily claimed that God had created all men equal, but they were no longer concerned to impose any specific version of deist or Christian doctrine as the basis of a sound commonwealth. This was a more profound and permanent break with the past than anything achieved in 1789, and was sustained without the morally destructive device of the Terror, which rejected the essential spirit of 'enlightenment'. The assumption that the Protestant churches and other forms of Christianity should have no direct political power, that a republican United States of America should be created with no official commitment to a particular form of Christianity, was accepted without much resistance. This was a sign of a growing acceptance of the 'enlightened' view, that the toleration of several unofficial forms of Christianity was better for the social system than the imposition of a single form by the state. In practice, there was a de facto Protestant hegemony in the new United States that lasted well into the 20th century, and which did not depend upon the authority of the state.

The French revolutionaries, on the other hand, retained the belief of their monarchist predecessors that the ideal state should be reflected in an ideal ecclesia. At one stage they tried to 'reform' the French Catholic Church, at another to introduce the worship of a Supreme Being. Van Kley argues that a central tragedy of the French Revolution was that Roman Catholicism was driven into adopting a role on the right of post-revolutionary European politics. Neither the Vatican nor the French Catholic Church could accept either the Jacobin assertion of lay independence from clerical authority, or the implication that in the modern state

Christianity should continue only as part of the individual's private life. The anti-Enlightenment religious and political tradition, which caricatured the Enlightenment as a conspiracy of intellectuals and Freemasons against God, his church, and monarchical government, may be dated from the 1790s, and became as important as the 'liberal individualism' against which it raged.

Important as these developments turned out to be, one should not allow one's interpretation of 18th-century religion to be dominated by the history of the French Revolution. A new, relatively optimistic view of human nature, at odds with the pessimistic side of the Christian tradition, became widespread both inside and outside the churches in the course of the century and survived the excesses of the Jacobins. Those who talked about an 'enlightened age' were claiming that Europeans now knew more and saw more clearly than their predecessors, and where science was concerned this was true. The French naturalist, Georges-Louis Buffon, for example, was already examining the evidence that suggested that the world as it was might not have been created by divine agency all of a piece and not very long ago, as Christian teaching had maintained, but had developed, both in geological and biological terms, over a vast space of time. The classical argument for the existence of God from design, which argued from order in the world to a supernatural designer, was sharply criticized by David Hume in the *Dialogues Concerning Natural Religion* (published posthumously in 1779), and although the Anglican theologian, William Paley, in his *Natural Theology* (1802), produced a very popular restatement of the belief that the universe could not have occurred by accident, a future containing Darwin, Marx, and Nietzsche's exultant 'There is no such thing as purpose—we invented purpose' was not far away.

Nevertheless, the fact that the churches seemed to be losing support in the 18th century does not oblige one to think in terms of a one-way secularizing process of modernizing 'enlightenment'. There were those in the churches who set out to revive traditional beliefs and practices, and others who wanted to reform religious institutions along lines suggested by 'enlightened' influences. In

Italy, for example, in the 1780s the Habsburg duke of Tuscany, Leopold, briefly gave state support to the would-be reformer, Scipione de Ricci, bishop of Pistoia in northern Italy. The synod of Pistoia in 1786, the high point of 'enlightened' influence in Roman Catholicism before the French Revolution, protested against parish missions, a characteristic Jesuit method of seeking to revive local religion by bringing into the parish powerful and ultimately centralizing forces from outside. On the other hand, the Synod was as much ducal as episcopal when it proposed to shift power in the church from the centralizing Vatican and the ubiquitous male and female orders to national churches in which the dynamic role would be that of the local parish priest. In the parish church there would be one plain altar, and, in a flight of fierce reaction against contemporary church architecture and decoration, the role of statuary would be reduced to a minimum; ideally, the mass would be said in the vernacular and the congregation would always communicate. One is suddenly looking at proposals which, while not in themselves 'enlightened', shared something of the 'enlightened' search for personal, existential certainty (both Diderot and Rousseau come to mind here); proposals which would play their part in the slow formation of an effective Catholic reform movement, whose breakthrough came at Vatican II.

This was a radical ecclesiastical reaction to the problems of 18th-century cultural change, and one sees something similar in the unsuccessful attempt made in England in 1772 to relax compulsory clerical subscription to the Anglican foundation-document, the Thirty-Nine Articles. In German Protestantism, on the other hand, there was more emphasis on the application of historical criticism to the documentary basis of Christianity as such. Johann Semler historicized the development of the biblical canon and so weakened its authority; and Samuel Reimarus, whose work was posthumously published by Lessing himself, showed once and for all how it was possible to argue that the text of the NT was made up of different layers of material, not all of which were even aimed at the same audience. Reimarus left the professional study of the life of Jesus in permanent disarray, but at the same time unintentionally offered 'radical' Christians a way of remaining within a Protestant culture.

These 18th-century solutions to the problems set by the Enlightenment had as yet no widespread support. In the *Analogy of Religion*, however, Joseph Butler produced a subtle and long-lasting restatement of orthodox theology. He started from the argument that 'natural religion', the alternative theological system that 18th-century Enlightenment theists offered, could not cope with 'the wretched state of the world', which was 'in ruin'. Butler argued that human repentance, the deist response to the moral requirements of the creator, was simply not enough, that one must accept the revelation of the NT, confirmed by the miraculous history of Christianity, that it needed divine intervention and the propitiatory sacrifice of Christ to restore creation. The argument from the 'ruined' state of the world was and remains emotionally powerful, and Butler's willingness to speak of Christ's redemptive acts as a mystery which we could not fully understand added to his appeal. John Wesley, on the other hand, while he was more intellectually conservative than Butler, was emotionally much less restrained: he moved beyond general ideas of repentance and redemption to the possibility of men and women being so utterly transformed in an individual experience of 'the power of the Spirit' that they might be described as being in a state of 'Christian perfection'.

When the German philosopher, Immanuel Kant, summed up in the 1790s what he took to be the essence of 'enlightenment', he described it as the individual's achievement of maturity, that is, of having the courage to think for oneself. In religious terms, this meant not only rejecting the churches' demand for conformity to a particular theological tradition, a demand still sometimes backed by the power of the state, but also refusing to submit to the emotional pressures that Kant saw at work in the Protestant Pietism of his day. Whereas John Wesley encouraged his followers to expect a conscious experience of divine power as the confirmation of the truth of Christianity, Kant argued that right conduct was the essence of religion, and dismissed what we might now call 'popular religion', whether Protestant or Catholic (*Religion within the Limits of Reason Alone*, 1794). His belief that one could trust one's understanding of the moral nature of the universe more safely than one could trust one's alleged religious experience, whether in the eucharistic service or in the revival meeting, that one's 'moral sense' was a more reliable guide than one's 'religious sense', set out a position on which one side of nineteenth-century humanist western culture was to rely heavily. Kant did not settle the argument. The idea that human beings are capable of an intuitive or mystical apprehension of a supernatural order was not so easily swept aside, either in philosophy, theology, or popular religion.

Romanticism reversed the trend, preferring existential faith to scepticism, distinguishing, rightly or wrongly, imagination from science. At the same time, however, the release of social, economic, and intellectual energy which had been reflected in self-conscious talk of 'enlightenment' continued to transform both society and the environment, and so confirmed the importance which the 18th century attached to unrestricted scientific investigation. As Hans Blumenberg has said (1966), what was losing plausibility was the Christian doctrine of providence.

In the 18th century it became clear that Christianity as the source of very specific theological world-views and ethical systems no longer dominated the intellectual life of western culture. Nevertheless, and despite the sociopolitical shocks of the American and French Revolutions, the churches emerged from apparent decline with renewed determination in the 19th century. Some of the sources of this recovery may be found in the part played by women in the 18th-century churches and, more broadly, in popular religion. But whatever the source, already before 1800 there were clear signs of the fresh missionary campaigns that would carry both Roman Catholic and Protestant Christianity all over the world in the following hundred years.

Adorno, T. W., and Horkheimer, M., *Dialectic of the Enlightenment* (1947), ET (1972).

Blumenberg, H., *The Legitimacy of the Modern Age* (1966), ET (1983).

Bolton, C. A., *Church Reform in 18th Century Italy (The Synod of Pistoia 1786)* (1969).

Butler, J., *The Analogy of Religion Natural and Revealed, to the Constitution and Course of Nature* (1874).

Byrne, J., *Glory, Jest and Riddle: Religious Thought in the Enlightenment* (1996).

Carroll, M. P., *Madonnas that Maim: Popular Catholicism in Italy since the Fifteenth Century* (1992).

Champion, J. A. I., *The Pillars of Priestcraft Shaken: The Church of England and its Enemies* (1992).

Chartier, Roger, *The Cultural Origins of the French Revolution*, ET (1991).

Chatellier, L., *The Europe of the Devout: The Catholic Reformation and the Formation of a New Society* (1987), ET (1989).

Delumeau, J., *Catholicism between Luther and Voltaire* (1971), ET (1977).

Diderot, D., *Supplément au Voyage de Bougainville* (1796), in *Œuvres*, ed. A. Billy (1951).

Dupront, A., *L. A. Muratori et la société européenne des pré-lumières* (1976).

Furbank, P. N., *Diderot: A Critical Biography* (1992).

Gay, P., *The Enlightenment: An Interpretation: The Rise of Modern Paganism* (1967).

Haakonssen, K. (ed.), *Enlightenment and Religion: Rational Dissent in Eighteenth-Century Britain* (1996).

Harrison, P., *'Religion' and Religions in the English Enlightenment* (1990).

Hume, D., *The Natural History of Religion*, ed. H. E. Root (1957).

Koselleck, R., *Critique and Crisis: Enlightenment and the Pathogenesis of Modern Society* (1959), ET (1988).

Labrousse, E., *Bayle* (1983).

Locke, J., *The Reasonableness of Christianity*, ed. I. T. Ramsey (1958).

Pailin, D. A., *Attitudes to Other Religions: Comparative Religion in Seventeenth and Eighteenth Century England* (1984).

Pocock, J. G. A., 'Clergy and Commerce: The Conservative Enlightenment in England', in *Eta dei Lumi: studia storice sul settecento Europeo in onore di F. Venturi* (1985).

Porter R., and Teich, M. (eds.), *The Enlightenment in National Context* (1981).

Sharpe, James, *Instruments of Darkness: Witchcraft in England 1550–1750* (1996).

Toland, J., *Christianity not Mysterious*, ed. G. Gawlick (1964).

Ugrinsky, A. (ed.), *Lessing and the Enlightenment* (1986).

Van Kley, Dale K., *The Religious Origins of the French Revolution: From Calvin to the Civil Constitution 1560–1791* (1996).

Vovelle, M., *Piété baroque et déchristianisation en Provence au xviii siècle: Les Attitudes devant la mort d'après les clauses des testaments* (1973).
Ward, W. R., *The Protestant Evangelical Awakening* (1992).

XII

CONFIDENCE AND QUESTIONS
The 19th century

❦ + ❦

Claude Welch

THE CHRISTIAN THEOLOGICAL ENTERPRISE IN EUROPE and America in the 19th century was a scene of changes unparalleled since the 16th-century Reformations, changes that set the problems and prefigured most of the directions for theologies in the 20th century. In socio-historical terms, despite the continuing secularization of the west, the century was notable for the emergence of a powerful Protestant foreign missionary enterprise, for popular Catholic revival on the Continent, and for such distinctive movements in North America as Mormonism and Christian Science. But Catholic and Protestant *theologies* alike were deeply troubled as well as creative, characterized by quite new modes of the struggle with Enlightenment criticism and a rapidly changing social order, as well as by powerful internal tensions between 'liberal' and 'conservative'.

For the beginning of the century, one naturally thinks of Schleiermacher, the founder of an epoch, whose *Speeches on Religion to its Cultured Despisers* appeared in 1799, and of the contemporary work of Hegel, Schelling (who was especially important for Catholicism), and Coleridge. Immediately in the background of their ventures were Kant's critical philosophy, the French Revolution, and the Napoleonic wars, whose shadows extended long into the century and were important for Roman Catholic and Protestant thought alike. There were independent creative moments elsewhere, notably in Britain and America, but the century's astonishing burst of vitality in the German faculties reverberated throughout the theological world. Eastern Orthodox Christianity was hardly participant in novel modes of religious thought, except in Russia, where the Christian philosopher Soloviev and the profoundly religious novelists Dostoevsky and Tolstoy have to be noted.

The theological dramas of the century can usefully be looked at as taking place on three broad and overlapping, almost concentric, stages. The most inclusive, for Catholic and Protestant thought alike in consequence of the Enlightenment, reflects the continuing struggle of the church(es) within the larger society. This framed a network of controversies about the nature of the church: about authority within it, its status and rights in relation to the state, and its responsibilities in relation to an increasingly industrialized society, a concern which culminated in 'social gospels' at the end of the century.

Overlaid on this broad scene were restatements of the fundamental nature of the theological enterprise, after the shocks to traditional theology from Pietism and the Enlightenment. New conceptions emerged most radically among Protestants. In Catholicism the problem was reflected in a new phase of debates over the relation of faith and reason, leading eventually to Vatican I and the modernist conflict. Correlated with questions of theological method were important problems in conceptualizing the relation between God and world.

Equally critical for the reconception of theology was the emergence of a new kind of historical consciousness, perhaps the most decisive theological development of the century, focusing particularly on the quest for the historical Jesus but also including the whole history of Christianity and its relation to other religious traditions. By the end of the century historical questions were at the centre of debate for both Catholics and Protestants.

🗡 The question of the church and society

At the beginning of the century, Napoleon drastically reordered the religio-political scene through the destruction of the prince-bishoprics and the reshuffling of the boundaries of the German states to include mixed Catholic and Protestant populations. This meant that the principle of the Peace of Augsburg (1555), that the religion of a state should be the religion of its ruler, was no longer viable. In France the Concordat of 1801 laid the ground for new ways of relating the papacy to the body of the faithful, particularly through the appointment of bishops. Napoleon's temporary annexation of the papal states (1809) and the exile of Pope Pius VII (1809–12) actually increased the prestige of the papacy and gave an impetus to 'popular ultramontanism' and the emergence of the papal title 'His Holiness'. However, along with spreading religious indifferentism and rising nationalisms, these actions also indicated threats to the existence of the papacy and of the Catholic church itself.

At the start of the century, movements to assert local authority as against that of the papacy were still significant. Known as Gallicanism in France, Febronianism in the German-speaking world, and Cisalpinism in Britain, they were modes of 'Catholic Enlightenment' urging the Catholic Church toward decentralization in structure and eclecticism in thought. But as the century wore on, especially after the restoration in 1814 of the Society of Jesus and the shift of intellectual gravity to the Gregorian University in Rome, the power of ultramontanism grew rapidly. It was coupled (especially by Pope Pius IX after the shock of the revolutions of 1848) with a new effort to maintain the rights and freedom of the church, tending to the development of a Catholic 'subculture' as a defence against the onslaughts of modernity, or what was called 'liberalism' in Pius's *Syllabus of Errors* (1864). Its resistance to various secular intrusions upon the church's rights, especially in regard to education and the family as well as internal church affairs, was coupled with rejections of so-called rationalism at several levels. This was carried further (especially in the First Vatican Council, and in Pope Leo XIII's encyclical *Aeterni Patris*, 1879) with the establishment of the philosophy of Thomas Aquinas as the great model for Catholic thought, both for theology and for the ordering of society as a whole. Political and theological questions were thoroughly intertwined in these developments. For example, Vatican I was able to deal only with the question of faith and reason (in a Thomistic way) and with the infallibility of the pope before being interrupted by the Franco-Prussian War.

Quite other ways of reasserting the rights of the church and defining its authority could be found in the form of a strict Lutheran Confessionalism, shaped in the mid-century by Löhe, Stahl, and others, and in the Oxford Movement in England, after 1833. The German Confessionalists were committed to the maintenance of state churches (throne and altar together). In this regard it is significant that after the death of Schleiermacher the Prussian king had pressed for the appointment of a 'believing' theologian as his successor at Berlin, to deliver the church from 'rationalism'. Such concern to preserve orthodoxy was also present in a milder way in the German pietist revivals and the religious-experience orientation of the Erlangen school.

The demand of the Oxford Movement, on the contrary, was for freedom of the church from state control, on the grounds of its ancient traditions and divinely established authority, in continuity with the apostolic succession. The American experiment of the separation of church and state was unique, being peculiarly related to the pluralism of the US. It was widely noted, even wistfully viewed by an occasional early 19th-century Catholic thinker, for example the Tübingen school's von Drey and the Cisalpine John Lingard, and enthusiastically appreciated by the German Catholic Hermann Schell at the end of the century, but it was not emulated in Europe or Britain. The final separation of church and state in France in 1905 was quite different. Perhaps the most dramatic proposal about church and state was the contention of the highly original 'speculative' theologian, Richard Rothe of Heidelberg, that Christianity should be freed from the church, whose previously assumed roles should be taken over by a secular-ethical culture. Though understandably never endorsed by any church, by the end of the 19th century Rothe's view could be seen as prophetic of the actual situation.

The Marxist critique of the church, especially after the *Communist Manifesto* of 1848, occasioned widely varying theological responses to the emerging industrial social order. On the negative side, these included intransigent opposition both to communist theory and to the programmes of the Social Democrats, a hostility represented by the main line of German Protestant theology (even Harnack thought the church had no responsibility to speak on economic matters) and, apart from the outstanding exception of Bishop Ketteler of Mainz (1811–77), by most Catholic social thought until Leo XIII's *Rerum Novarum* (1891). This became the charter for a Catholic labour movement and for social Catholicism in general.

More positive reactions to Marxism ranged from the mild (and sentimentally utopian) Christian Socialism of F. D. Maurice and his associates in Britain in the early 1850s, through later vigorous outcries against social injustices, to the radical religious socialism in late 19th-century Swiss Protestantism (Kutter and Ragaz) which hailed the despised Social Democrats for doing what the church ought itself to have been doing. Walter Rauschenbusch in America proposed that theology should be revised so as to be adequate for a social gospel. By the end of the century, Protestant social gospels were flourishing in Britain and in America, proposing economic and social reforms, from merely palliative measures that would moderate the worst abuses of industrial society to full-scale attacks on capitalism as incompatible with the Christian gospel.

New views of the theological task

Kant's emphasis on the constitutive role of the mind in all knowledge was reflected in a new and decisive 'turn to the subject' at the cutting edge of 19th-century theology. The religious subject, its point of view, its cognitive structures, its 'interest', its willing and choosing, had to be consciously and systematically recognized as present at the starting-point of theological reflection.

There was continuity here with the Enlightenment confidence in the human. The difference is the rejection of the 18th century's rationalism. This was classically expressed in Schleiermacher's proposal, influenced by Romanticism and his own early exposure to Moravian Pietism, that *Gefühl*, feeling (or, later, in the *Glaubenslehre*, the 'feeling of utter dependence') is the heart of the religious defined as the deepest level of self-consciousness and awareness, in contrast to the Enlightenment preoccupation with beliefs and morals.

Hegel also took this inward turn, although his view of the self was quite different. He despised the idea of utter dependence. He posited an essentially reasoning and thinking self, but enlarged the idea of the rational to incorporate both the Romantic quest for unity and universality and the dialectic of movement, of subjective and objective moments, in thought and in history. By thus offering a dynamic model of the self, divine or human, Hegel thought he could secure the traditional doctrines of Incarnation and Trinity marginalized by Schleiermacher. Not altogether unlike Hegel's idea of reason (though more Schellingian in its roots) was Coleridge's notion of reason as the organ of the 'supersensuous', recalling the Cambridge Platonists. But this reason again transcended Enlightenment fixation on the phenomenal world of sense perception, represented among Coleridge's contemporaries by Bentham and Paley. Reason was to include imagination and will, even the courage to venture beyond the provable. Similarly, Coleridge prophetically redefined the authority of scripture as its power to speak to the deepest needs of the self.

The turn to the self was reflected in many other ways: in Emerson's focus on religious sentiment; in F. D. Maurice's rejection of every 'system' and his insistence on the partiality and distortion of all apprehensions; in Horace Bushnell's theory of religious language; supremely in Kierkegaard's recognition of truth as subjectivity; in Albrecht Ritschl's assertion that religious knowledge consists in 'judgments of value'; in the French liberal Auguste Sabatier's emphasis on psychological religion; in William James's account of the will to believe and his pragmatic theory of truth; in Cardinal Newman's 'illative sense'; in the Catholic modernist George Tyrrell's conception of doctrine; and in Ernst Troeltsch's embracing of 'relativism' and of the truth of Christianity 'for us'.

Thus the idea of revelation itself had to be reconsidered and the former confidence in its truths was dissolved. The question was not *whether* revelation was to be accepted, but rather *what* does 'revelation' mean? And so the old apologetics that took prophecy and miracle as warrants for 'revealed truth' had to be abandoned.

The 19th-century anthropological turn took its most extreme form in Ludwig Feuerbach's internal critique of theology, in which 'religion' is to be taken with the utmost seriousness, but its talk about God has to be understood as a projection of human attributes and an expression of human wishes (the *Essence of Christianity*, 1840). Thus theology *is* anthropology. Feuerbach insisted that he wanted to celebrate the human, real, sensuous person. His projection theory was later taken up by Freud in the idea of religion as illusion, and his affirmation of the human was to be reflected in Friedrich Nietzsche's proclamation of the death of God and his bitter polemic against Christianity's slave morality.

More generally in Protestant liberal theologies, which seemed to be sweeping all before them by the end of the century, the ideas of revelation and of human discovery merged, with religious experience identified as the basis for all theology. A similar appeal to experience was presupposed by Tyrrell, marking a radical change from the earlier Roman Catholic tradition found in the faith/reason discussions, increasingly dominated by the Thomistic view.

Not often so explicitly stated, but widely implicit in the later 19th century's idea of the theological enterprise, was another of Schleiermacher's proposals. In the *Brief Outline on the Study of Theology* (1811; 1830) he argued that dogmatics, or systematic theology, has to be understood as the articulation of the *contemporary* religious consciousness of the church, running parallel to 'church statistics' (i.e. sociology of religion). Thus emerged a new way of ordering the theological enterprise, contrary both to the tradition of the Protestant scholastics and to the 'natural theology' of the 17th and 18th centuries. The theological venture could then be defended on the basis either of its independence and the *sui generis* nature of the religious (Schleiermacher), or of its unity with the whole of human experience and its embodiment of western culture (Hegel, and speculative and idealist theologies generally). Those contrasting perspectives provide an illuminating typology for the century's philosophies of religion.

Intimately related to the reconsideration of the nature of the theological task was the critique of 'supernaturalism', with a new stress instead on immanence in conceptions of the relation of God and the world. The older ideas of theism, dominated by divine transcendence (and carried to an extreme in deism), were replaced in both Schleiermacher and Hegel by what the 20th century would call panentheism, where God is not identified totally with the cosmos (pantheism) but includes it. More radical immanentism was to emerge in Emerson's light-hearted and happy celebration of the divinity of man, leading in the direction of a thoroughgoing religious naturalism, and in the later Strauss's more heavy-handed evolutionary monism (*The Old Faith and the New*, 1872).

Parallel to these tendencies, traditional conceptions of divine immutability began to be criticized both in a prophetic essay on the subject by the mid-century mediating thinker, Isaak Dorner, and (though for somewhat different reasons) in the emergence of several kenotic christologies in mid-century Germany and late-century Anglicanism. Some of that critique laid the ground for 20th-century process theologies and conceptions of a limited God. In William James's pluralistic universe, for instance, the suffocating absolute of idealist philosophy is replaced by a world with real evil and a God genuinely engaged in the struggle for good. These moves were vigorously opposed by Protestant orthodoxy and by the main line of Catholic theology. The charge of 'immanentism' was to be a central theme in Pope Pius X's condemnation of modernism in 1907.

The struggle over Darwin and the theory of evolution can be viewed partly as a critical focus of the question of how God relates to the world. Certainly in the relation of science and theology, the 19th was Darwin's century. The theological response to *The Origin of Species* (1859) has been often misconstrued. It did not represent a warfare of science and religion, except in the minds of some interpreters. For the best-known of those, the real conflict was primarily between a new 'scientific history', especially in biblical studies, and institutional religious (especially Roman Catholic) intransigence. There was initially little of the explosion that was to come with the fundamentalist anti-evolution campaign of the 1920s in America, though towards the end of the 19th century Darwin was taken up as ammunition by the Social Democrats in Germany in a battle they were already waging against religion in the name of socialism and materialism.

The variety of serious theological reactions (Catholic as well as Protestant) to Darwin in the 19th century was quite as complicated as the scientific responses (among the latter, Neo-Lamarckism was as widely accepted as Darwin's theory until after 1900). Religious reactions ranged from bitter hostility in some theologians because of the apparent exclusion of design and the denial of human uniqueness, through qualified acceptance (at least in relation to the development of the human body), to a hearty embrace of evolution as a description of the way God has worked immanently in the world. A God who is only an occasional visitor is an impossible conception: either we banish God altogether or we believe in his immanence in nature from end to end, to summarize Aubrey Moore's classic statement in *Lux Mundi* (1889). Towards the end of the century the idea of evolution (more in a Spencerian than a Darwinian form) could even be heralded as the new paradigm for understanding all things religious and cultural. Martin Kähler claimed that it was easy for German theologians to become Darwinians because 'we were already Hegelians and Hegel anticipated the whole of Darwin'.

In fact, it was conservatives like Charles Hodge in America and Otto Zöckler in Germany who were most attentive to Darwin's own position, which they took to be simply contrary to the biblical teaching about the origin of humanity. One sees here orthodoxy's tendency to the all-or-nothing view, a way of thinking operating at many levels. These range from Newman's sophisticated commitment to 'dogma' and his contention in the *Apologia pro Vita Sua* (1864) that there was no real middle-ground between Catholic truth and rationalism, to some simplistic fundamentalist objections to any 'higher criticism' on the grounds that, like being only 'a little pregnant', being only a little doubtful of scriptural inerrancy opened the door to scepticism and atheism.

✍ The historical question

The publication of D. F. Strauss's *The Life of Jesus Critically Examined* (1835) was an event of the greatest magnitude both theologically and politically. The work aroused a storm of controversy in Germany, a 'panic-stricken terror' according to the leading contemporary Protestant church historian, F. C. Baur, and it eventually destroyed Strauss's chances of an academic theological career. Politically the work was welcomed by the new left-wing Hegelians as implying radical democratic politics in its conflict with the establishment. The book, translated into English by George Eliot, was so shocking to British sensibilities that, apart from the *Westminster Review* liberals and S. T. Coleridge's posthumous *Confessions of an Inquiring Spirit* (1840), extensive and open debate did not take place in England until the publication of *Essays and Reviews*, a highly controversial engagement with Strauss by a group of more liberal Anglicans, in 1860. In Roman Catholic circles, the new critical perspectives did not come to centre-stage until the modernist controversy at the end of the century.

Strauss proposed a 'mythological' view of the origin of the gospel stories as unconscious poetic products of the early Christian community, which applied the more general idea of humanity united with divinity to the one human figure of Jesus. Both supernaturalist and rationalist interpretations of the gospels were quite implausible in view of the contradictions and repetitions in the texts. Supernaturalism conflicted with the canons of physical science, a consistent chronology, and with any conceivable psychology of Jesus' life. Rationalist explanations simply left out the content of religion, the 'divine'. The question for Strauss as a Hegelian was not whether there was a deep unity between the human and the divine—Hegel stood for that—but whether historical science could justify the identification of the divine–human Christ-figure of orthodoxy with the individual person Jesus.

Strauss thus inaugurated the modern era in critical NT study, which for the most part in the 19th century was the history of German criticism. Higher criticism developed alongside extensive efforts to establish the Greek text of the NT through analysis of the ancient manuscripts, many newly discovered. At the outset, the gospel of John, on which the tradition (including even Schleiermacher) had depended so much, had to be rejected as a reliable historical source. This laid the groundwork for subsequent debates over the relation of the Synoptic Gospels, quickly leading to the thesis of the priority of Mark and to the two-source hypothesis (Mark and Q, a sayings source) for the gospels of Luke and Matthew, an explanation dominant by the end of the century. By that time too, the Graf–Wellhausen theory that posited four source documents underlying the Pentateuch had won the day in Britain and America as well as in Germany, undermining claims of Mosaic authorship.

What were the results? One was that the attempt to construct a scientific 'life of Jesus' from the gospel records had to be given up as impossible. As Martin Kähler put it, 'we have no sources for a biography of Jesus of Nazareth which measure up to the standards of contemporary historical science', but only 'a vast field strewn with the fragments of various traditions'. The question was only partly 'what can be known about Jesus?', and there even the argument that there was no such historical person could resurface.

The question was equally whether the figure who could be known is appropriate for the faith of modern human beings.

Thus a second result was extended debate over the nature and presuppositions of historical study. Kähler, in his famous 1892 lecture, 'The so-called Jesus of history and the historic biblical Christ', first proposed the distinction between the *historisch* and the *geschichtlich*. The former indicates 'scientific' historical study that abstracts from the presuppositions of faith and operates on the principles of causality and psychological analogy in human experience. The latter characterizes historical work shaped from the outset by faith's confession that Jesus is Lord and that the divine cannot be separated from the human in the gospel stories. This latter kind of history alone is appropriate to the gospels as proclamation.

A third result was the rediscovery of the apocalyptic in Jesus' teaching about the Kingdom of God, a theme emphasized by Strauss but recovered at the end of the century by Johannes Weiss and Albert Schweitzer. The apocalyptic interpretation was wholly unacceptable, for example, to the leading Protestant liberal of the day, Adolf Harnack, as making quite impossible the essence of the kingdom as the rule of God in the hearts and souls of individuals. The eschatological question was to generate the sharpest tensions in Protestant thought for a century. The apocalyptic view was taken up by the Catholic modernists Loisy and Tyrrell, though with vastly different conclusions from their Protestant counterparts. For them, the church was the appropriate fulfilment of the idea of the heavenly kingdom in Jesus' teaching. To say that 'Jesus foretold the kingdom, and it was the church that came', rather than showing the betrayal of Jesus' message as Harnack thought, simply expresses the necessity of the church for the proclamation of the gospel. This attempt to justify the development of Catholicism was hardly acceptable to Rome. Loisy was one of the principal targets in Pope Pius X's condemnation of modernism, and that event, along with the uniformly conservative decisions of the newly reconstituted Biblical Commission (1903), was to shut down the promising beginnings of

Roman Catholic critical biblical study and drive it underground for half a century.

Three related dimensions of the new historical consciousness had emerged by the end of the century: the *Religionsgeschicht-lichesschule* (history of religions school) looking at religion as a human phenomenon, the reconsideration of the history of the church and theology, and much more broadly the new study of comparative religion. All of these were reflected in the work of Ernst Troeltsch, as well as of his Catholic contemporary Hermann Schell, who was particularly interested in the work of the great theorist and translator of Eastern religious texts, Max Müller.

The *Religionsgeschichtlichesschule* was especially important for biblical studies. Biblical religion had to be seen as fully a part of general religious history, intimately related to its socioreligious surroundings and influenced by them. This applied to the emergence of early Christianity as a syncretistic movement out of a syncretistic Judaism, as well as, for example, to the creation stories in relation to Babylonian creation myths.

Christian history, especially its theology, had also to be reassessed. For Harnack, in his famous history of dogma, it was to be seen as the corruption of the simple gospel of Jesus by the incorporation of Greek metaphysical categories ('Dogma, in its conception and its construction, is a work of the Greek spirit'), as well as by the emergence of Catholic institutionalism. Though his was an essentially 'ideological-dogmatic' kind of history, Harnack was quite aware of the interplay of social, political, and intellectual influences in the development of theology. But it was Troeltsch, notably in the classic *Social Teachings of the Christian Churches and Groups* (1912), who most clearly articulated the social conditioning of theological ideas and the pluralism within Christianity, so that 'church history' had to become a social history of Christianity, an 'essentially sociological-realistic-ethical' history.

In Troeltsch's lifelong concern with the question of the 'absoluteness' (or the finality) of Christianity, there came a kind of culmination of the 19th century's new recognition of the problem of the relationship between Christianity and other religions, in which the older attitude of exclusiveness and even intolerance was abandoned. Early in the century, the Romantic vision had freed the European mind to become not only curious about other people's religions but also appreciative of them as authentic expressions of the human experience. Both Schleiermacher and Hegel had partly reflected this change of spirit. But in the explosion of knowledge about other religions, including not only the great developed traditions of the Far East but also Egyptian, ancient Mediterranean, and 'primitive' or non-literate religion, a new kind of study of religion flourished by the end of the century. Here the early 19th century turn to the subject developed into an 'objective' study of religious subjectivity itself. This is seen in William James's *Varieties of Religious Experience* (1902), but also the extensive studies of pre-literate religiousness and the attempts to identify the earliest forms of the religious, whether in animism or totemism or even some 'high god' concepts. Frazer's *The Golden Bough* epitomizes the approach. Much of this reflection was dominated by evolutionary notions of development, which often reflected the optimism of the late century.

We owe to Troeltsch a classic formulation of the principles of historical enquiry: criticism (so that all historical judgements prove to be tentative), analogy (so that nothing can be exempted from analogy with our present experience of happenings), and correlation (in which everything is related to everything else). The final result had to be a relativism in which the most that can be said is that the truth of a religious view (in his case the Christian one) is its truth 'for us', inseparable from our particular sociocultural situation.

In sum, by the end of the 19th century one can see both in Protestant liberalism in its struggle with conservatism, and in the suppression of Roman Catholic modernism, unresolved tensions in all the major areas of concern: the relation of church and society; the nature of the theological enterprise and the 'truth' of its faith or the validity of its ethics; and the consequences of the new historical consciousness. These problems were to shape the efforts of the 20th century.

Barth, Karl, *Protestant Theology in the Nineteenth Century* (1946), ET (1972).

Berkhof, Hendrikus, *Two Hundred Years of Theology* (1989).

Chadwick, Owen, *The Secularization of the European Mind in the Nineteenth Century* (1975).

Fitzer, Joseph, *Romance and the Rock: Nineteenth-Century Catholics on Faith and Reason* (1989).

Livingston, James C., *Modern Christian Thought: From the Enlightenment to Vatican II* (1971).

McCool, Gerald A., *Nineteenth Century Scholasticism* (1989).

Misner, Paul, *Social Catholicism in Europe: From the Onset of Industrialization to the First World War* (1991).

O'Meara, Thomas F., *Church and Culture: German Catholic Theology, 1860–1914* (1991).

Pelikan, Jaroslav, *Christian Doctrine and Modern Culture (since 1700)* (1989).

Reardon, Bernard M. G., *Religious Thought in the Nineteenth Century* (1966).

Schoof, T. M., *A Survey of Catholic Theology, 1800–1970* (1970).

Smart, Ninian, *et al.* (eds.), *Nineteenth-Century Religious Thought in the West* (3 vols.; 1985). Extensive bibliographies.

Welch, Claude, *Protestant Thought in the Nineteenth Century* (2 vols.; 1972; 1985). Extensive bibliographies.

XIII

CONFLICT AND RAPPROCHEMENT
The 20th century

Adrian Hastings

IN THE WINTER TERM OF 1899–1900, ADOLPH HARNACK gave a series of open lectures in the University of Berlin on the nature of Christianity. They were attended by more than 600 students and their text was immediately published and translated into English. *What is Christianity?* went into many editions and, perhaps more than any other book, represents the quintessence of authoritative Christian thought at the start of the 20th century, the high point of liberal Protestant theology. Germany had dominated the field throughout the nineteenth century and Harnack personified that domination in several ways. As Rector of the University of Berlin as well as its Professor of Church History, and a member of the Royal Prussian Academy, he stood at the heart of the German academic, and indeed political, world. His immense learning and the clarity of his teaching made him personally extremely influential, so that many outstanding thinkers of the next generation had been his students. In 1900 he was 50 years old, at the height of his powers, and would continue to be a very active presence in the theological world for another 25 years. No one else so straddled the centuries. Nineteenth-century Germany had rewritten Christian theology as either philosophy of a post-Hegelian sort or as history. It was the latter approach that Harnack represented and it was so persuasive because it appeared to deal in convincing scholarly detail with the way Christianity had come to be, both in scripture and in the development of church history. It was 'scientific', a word Harnack regularly repeated (using it in its German sense of 'systematic'). His three-volume *History of Dogma* and related works outlined a view of Christianity whose main thrust it seemed hard to deny. Moreover, his was not a sceptical or secular viewpoint. It was an account of 'The Gospel', as he liked to call it, by a believer. But it was essentially 'scientific theology', that is to say 'critical-historical study', which led, he thought, to a view of Christ that could and should lead to faith in the God and Father of Christ. For Harnack, in theology science had to come first but good science would lead to true faith.

He thought that true Christianity must be centred on the Father whom Jesus preached, and not on Jesus himself. He had little time for any of the dogmatic developments he had re-searched so skilfully. They almost all led in the wrong direction. The true Jesus was an ethical teacher whose nature wonderfully reflected that of God and whose guidance could lead the modern world along the paths of a liberal Protestantism. It was essentially spiritual and other-worldly, with no political message whatsoever but not, Harnack believed, anti-worldly. His was an optimistic interpretation of religion suited to an optimistic age and it did not challenge his own views, which combined confidence in the advance of civilization with conservative, even nationalist, politics. Christianity represented the very best in human religion, no less but little more.

The influence of Harnack was enormous on the thousands of pastors who attended his lectures over the years, but his own Lutheran Church could not accept a teaching that denied the strictly miraculous, including the Virgin Birth, the Resurrection, and Ascension, as well as the dogmatic value of the credal affirm-ations of Nicaea and Chalcedon. The Supreme Council of the Evangelical Church had vetoed his appointment to the Berlin Chair, but the veto had been overruled by the emperor with the support of the faculty. Nevertheless, the church denied him official recognition throughout his life.

Much the same tension between a near-consensus of the learned theological world and the authority of the church could be found elsewhere. In 1906 the young William Temple, son of an archbishop of Canterbury, on a visit to Berlin, wrote back to the bishop of Oxford about his hesitations in regard to the Virgin Birth and the Resurrection. The bishop of Oxford declined to ordain him, although two years later Temple claimed to have come to a sufficient degree of acceptance of both beliefs to be ordained by Randall Davidson, the archbishop of Canterbury and a friend of his father. A few years later (1912) he contributed to *Foundations*, a volume of essays by young Oxford scholars that produced a great deal of tension between ecclesiastical and scholarly viewpoints, symptomatic of a far wider unease between theological thought, traditional belief, and church authority, whether Protestant, Anglican, or Catholic. In North America the anti-liberal reaction in these same years produced a series of tracts entitled *The Fundamentals* (1910–15), giving its name to the fundamentalism that would remain throughout the century a principal component of American Christianity.

Nowhere else, however, was the tension so acute as in the Catholic Church. It was inevitable that Catholic scholars in France and elsewhere should have shared in the scientific reformulation of church history and biblical studies. Mgr. Duchesne (1843–1922), a professor in Paris and then director of the French School in Rome, was nearly as distinguished an early church historian as Harnack. It was inevitable too that the gap between this growing scholarly consensus and popular devotion should become ever wider: the multitude of dubious relics, the forest of indulgences, the incredible lives of saints, all cried out for the scathing criticism of historians more interested in precise evidence than in encouraging participation in local feasts and pilgrimages. The trouble, however, was that such popular devotions had been built into the official ecclesiastical system and an attack on, say, the belief that the Holy House of Loreto had sailed through the air from Nazareth in the 13th century to settle down in Italy was judged at least 'offensive to pious ears'.

Duchesne's three-volume history of the early church was placed on the Index in 1912.

The movement of Catholic theological renewal, however, went much further than a criticism of such things. It very largely accepted the biblical and early church analysis of Harnack. Maybe Jesus never instituted the sacrament of baptism, maybe Moses did not write the Pentateuch, all that and much else might be accommodated within a horizon of history in which what mattered was a bond of development, guided by the Holy Spirit, but shaped by the culture and needs of the age. When Alfred Loisy wrote his *L'Évangile et l'Église* (1902) he saw himself as replying to Harnack from an essentially contrary ecclesiastical standpoint, grounded in Newman's idea of doctrinal development, rather than as adopting his viewpoint. While they were often nearer than claimed, the contrast in principle was a real one; but for church authority, especially in the Rome of Pius X and his secretary of state, Cardinal Merry del Val, all this was wholly unacceptable. Loisy and his like were undermining many basic Roman claims and opening the door to the abandonment of a great deal of doctrine and practice judged as the fruit of medieval superstition unacceptable to modernity. Loisy could in practice be as damning of the way dogma had actually developed as Harnack himself.

In reality, despite the condemnatory definition given in the encyclical *Pascendi*, there never was a coherent theory of modernism. There were simply a number of different people, scholars, theologians, thinkers of various sorts, many of them linked in friendship but seldom with quite the same ideas. They included the increasingly radical French priest Loisy, the Anglo-Irish Jesuit George Tyrrell, both arguably heretical enough, but also Friedrich von Hügel, an aristocratic layman, and Tyrrell's close friend, a man as devout as he was learned, the Abbé Brémond, a historian of spirituality, and many others. Possible suspects were myriad. Even Mgr. Duchesne might be numbered among them. In July 1907 the Holy Office issued a decree *Lamentabili*, listing the errors of modernism and followed two months later by *Pascendi*, which presented a systematic account of what it described as the sum total of all the heresies, and pre-scribing the most rigorous methods to eradicate this threat to Catholicism, including an 'anti-modernist oath' to be taken by all bishops, ordinands, and university and seminary teachers.

While many suspected 'modernists' went to ground avoiding formal condemnation, Tyrrell's temperament required the oppos-ite approach and he accepted invitations from both *The Times* and the *Giornale d'Italia* to write articles criticizing the encyclical, an action equivalent to ecclesiastical suicide. He was excommuni-cated by papal orders and remained excommunicated until his death. In 1908, Cardinal Mercier of Malines wrote a Lenten pas-toral letter, upholding *Pascendi*, remarking somewhat smugly that Belgium was blessedly free of the modernist disease but going on to name Tyrrell as an English priest 'deeply imbued' with mod-ernism. He named no one else. Mercier's gratuitous mention of him in a Belgian pastoral prompted Tyrrell to write a small mas-terpiece, *Medievalism*, in six weeks. This was by no means the most important of his works: *Christianity at the Crossroads*, published post-humously, was considerably weightier. Tyrrell was not the most profound thinker in the modernist movement, nor its greatest scholar, but he was its most brilliant writer, with the ability to put his finger on the spot that hurt most, as well as the audacity to stand in the breach when almost everyone else was trying to es-cape attention.

Mercier denounced modernism by branding it a form of Protestantism, than which, it appeared, nothing could be worse: 'The Protestant nations [by which he meant particularly Germany, England, and the United States] are sick.' Their sickness lay, above all, in 'individualism' which he contrasted with the Catholic insistence upon 'authority'. Tyrrell replied that modern-ism was anything but Protestant and anything but individualistic; it insisted above all on a church which is Catholic because it is the community of many minds and cultures whereas, he declared, the ultramontanism of Vatican I and of Mercier himself was the true individualism because it had reduced the shaping of Christianity to a single individual, the pope. Tyrrell died little more than a year later, obstinately Catholic yet excommunicate, denied even burial in Catholic ground. Mercier's pastoral letter and Tyrrell's reply are important partly because Mercier was one of the most intellectual and forward-looking bishops in the Catholic Church, the protagonist and patron of the revival of scholasticism at Louvain, responsible twenty years later for the Malines Conversations with Anglicans. Yet his pastoral of 1908 shows clearly the inability of Catholic leadership to comprehend either modernism or the minimum requirements of historical science for theology.

The gap between ultramontane orthodoxy and the requirements of a modern (let alone modernist) theology seemed unbridgeable. Tyrrell was not mistaken in characterizing the religion of Mercier and Pius X, in contrast to his own admitted modernism, as 'medievalism'. The result was that *Pascendi* was followed by 25 years of exceptional intellectual aridity within Catholicism. Abbot Cuthbert Butler of Downside wrote to von Hügel in 1922 to explain why he had abandoned serious theological study:

> A priest can publish nothing without 'imprimatur'. The only freedom in Biblical things and the rest is that of a tram, to go ahead as fast as you like on rails, but if you try to arrive at any station not on the line, you are derailed . . . When the Biblical Commission got under way, and the *Lamentabili* and *Pascendi* were issued, I deliberately turned away from all this work—my being Abbot made it not apparent. (*Downside Review* (1979), 298–9).

Cuthbert Butler was hardly a radical. If he could find no other course theologically than to silence himself, there was indeed little room within a Catholicism lying beneath the shadow of the anti-modernist witch-hunt for any significant expression of Christian thought.

Loisy and Tyrrell had hoped to challenge Harnack's interpretation of Christianity in the name of Catholicism but were disqualified from doing so by their own church authority. He was, however, challenged in several other ways. The first and most finally decisive challenge was that produced by his friend and colleague, the philosopher of history, Ernst Troeltsch. Harnack was himself a devout believer. He held, quite simplistically, that scientific history must lead to religious faith, the faith he thought Jesus proclaimed in God's fatherhood and man's brotherhood. But Troeltsch realized that history as such could never found any absolute claim for Christianity in its particularity. One simply cannot establish faith on science, yet for Troeltsch as for Harnack there was no sound theology other than historicism. For Harnack, that remained enough to justify his faith but Troeltsch, to his own deep regret, saw ever more clearly as he approached the end of his life that it must signify the demise of Christianity. 'All I have been able to do for you', he remarked to a grateful student, 'is that I showed you the sunset of Christianity. When the sun has set, it still glows for a long time' (Pauck 1968: 92). A sunset may be inspiring enough, but for Troeltsch whether there would ever be another sunrise was quite uncertain.

Hardly less threatening was the challenge mounted by Albert Schweitzer's *Quest of the Historical Jesus* (1906; ET 1910). The challenge here was less to the central methodological cogency of the Harnackian view than to its content: the delineation of Jesus. Where Harnack believed that you could strip the historical Jesus of later christological, miraculous, and mythological accretions to arrive at a moral teacher wholly in accord with the sensibilities of late 19th-century Protestant Europe, Schweitzer powerfully concluded that Jesus' teaching was dominated by an eschatological conviction that the end was near, not at all what a post-Enlightenment Europe could find congenial. Schweitzer may have overstated his case, but he and numerous other scholars demonstrated how dangerous it is to be overconfident about the religious authority derivable from historicism.

Liberal Neo-Protestantism was challenged yet again by the fact of the First World War. Such appalling and pointless carnage undermined the comfortable and optimistic cultural context in which it had flourished and for which it could seem a sufficient theology. Moreover, while the public hegemony of Christianity had mostly survived in the western world up to this point, if in ever more emasculated form, it now largely collapsed, both politically and culturally. The dominant intellectual influences were almost ostentatiously non-Christian: Marx, Nietzsche, Freud, Frazer. Christian thought was pushed quite rapidly from the centre to the periphery of intelligent academic debate. In such a *bouleversement* of role, the comfortable, establishmentarian liberalism of a Harnack had lost its social point. Something a great deal more confrontational was called for. Hence the rise of 'dialectical theology', a term used to describe the work of a group who came to dominate the scene in the 1920s and 1930s, all of whom—if in very different ways—accentuated the gap between Christian believing and secular presuppositions rather than the continuities. Already as the war ended the most powerful challenge to the whole stream of Christian thought represented by Harnack had been mounted by one of his former students, the young Swiss theologian Karl Barth, in his commentary on Romans, first published in 1919 and then republished in greatly extended form in 1921, a work that, in the words of the Catholic Tübingen theologian Karl Adam, 'fell like a bomb on the playground of the theologians'. If it fell 'like a bomb' on the theologians, something else a few years earlier had fallen like a bomb on Barth. It was the letter published in August 1914 by ninety-three German intellectuals, including Harnack and almost the entire theological establishment, approving the Kaiser's war aims. For Barth that was a 'black day'. Of what conceivable use was a theology whose leading proponents could so behave? 'So far as I was concerned, there was no more future for the theology of the 19th century.'

Barth was, surely, the most powerful and influential theological mind of the 20th century. To Harnack, courteous gentleman as he was, especially when faced by a young friend, Barth's views were simply incomprehensible, 'naive biblicism'. In the famous and fascinating, if obscure, correspondence between them in 1923, one may pick out the dominant theme. If Jesus Christ stands at the centre of the gospel, how else, asked Harnack, 'can the basis for reliable and communal knowledge of this person be gained but through critical-historical study so that an imagined Christ is not put in place of the real one? What else beside scientific theology is able to undertake this study?' To which Barth replied that 'the "scientific character" of theology' involves 'the recollection that its object *was once subject* and must become that again and again'. The theologian must not begin by studying Paul or Luther as objects but by reliving their experience as subject. We accept the bible uncritically in faith as God's word but then find within it a profound rationality of its own. Barth developed this basic position in his study of Anselm's theology, *Fides quaerens intellectum*, of 1931. Faith has to come first. For Harnack, writing in 1928 near the end of his life, this constituted the intellectual suicide of theology: 'Barth's reversion to bibliolatry—even Calvin did not go so far—is a piece of scholarly and religious naivety which could only have won the temporary success that it has done at a period like ours, of general despair over reason and scholarship' (to Erik Peterson).

In his total rejection of natural theology, the insights of other religions, or religious experience, Barth was opposing himself not only to the central themes of 19th-century Protestantism but no less to Catholicism. His repudiation of a Thomist *analogia entis*— an analogy of being between creatures and creator allowing us to speak of God—became almost the hallmark of full Barthianism. And yet Barth grew far closer to Catholic theology than he realized, largely because he accepted a fundamental veracity in the gospels and because the christology that was central to his work included within it a strong ecclesiology.

If 'scientific theology' had to its own satisfaction undermined that veracity, leaving in Harnack's view the image of a wonderful God-filled man but in Schweitzer's that of a much mistaken eschatological enthusiast, how could one build a theology of any sort, strong enough to be preached not within the reverential portals of an established church but in the academic market-place against the mounting roar of Marxist, Communist, Nazi, and liberal atheist? Rudolf Bultmann was an almost exact contemporary of Barth. He reversed Harnack's position as decisively but in a very different direction. The 'Jesus of History' could not be known and did not matter. Even to bother about his historic character, beyond the one great *Daß* (that) he died and rose again, is a betrayal of faith. For the true Lutheran, all that need matter is the 'Christ of faith'. Bultmann, one of the greatest of biblical scholars, essentially accepted that scientific study of the NT left one with nothing but a tissue of 'myths' which needed to be 'demythologized' to reveal any message appropriate to the 20th century. But for him it had still to be a 'dialectical' message of faith, not reason. If such an exercise be accepted, it runs into problems in deciding what are the values left in place by demythologization. If it is personal 'commitment', then to what is one committed? Bultmann filled the content of a demythologized faith with the categories of current existentialism. While the power of his scholarship and engagement with such a gospel exercised a strong influence in his lifetime, it was a theology bound to wane when, with the passing of time, the content of his demythologized gospel itself proved as culturally dated as he believed the original gospel to have been.

Despite the comparable influence exercised by Paul Tillich, especially in the USA where he had fled from Nazi Germany, he too displayed the inherent problem of reinventing a workable Protestant theology, neither simply a matter of historical science nor yet almost ostentatiously anti-scientific. In fact the core of his attempt to correlate Christian belief with what was essentially a humanistic ethic and philosophy of history was not so different, as he himself recognized, from late 19th-century German 'scientific' theology as found in Ritschl or Troeltsch.

In his correspondence with Peterson in 1928, Harnack, reflecting upon the identity of Protestantism, distinguished between two elements within it: the one 'Schleiermacherism' including a larger 'illuminist and subjective current', the other 'the Catholic element in primitive Protestantism'. If the former had no future other than a beautiful sunset or sectarianism, then the latter was likely to renew its appeal. Effectively that is what was happening in Barth's case, with his attempt to construct a *Church* Dogmatics. The case for it would be strengthened by the recovery of intellectual vitality within the Catholic Church itself.

This recovery began to appear fairly cautiously after the traumas of anti-modernism. From Germany came the work of Karl

Adam at Tübingen. His *Das Wesen des Katholizismus* (ET, *The Spirit of Catholicism*, 1928), focusing on the church as Christ's mystical body, exercised a profound influence on a generation of Catholics worldwide. But the recovery was at first most manifest on the philosophical front and due especially to two remarkable French laymen, Jacques Maritain and Étienne Gilson. It was they, building undoubtedly on the work of other scholars and thinkers, who chiefly managed to make of the revival of 'scholasticism' so emphatically required by Catholic authority something other than a piece of 'medievalism'. The homogenized scholasticism of the seminaries and Catholic universities appeared at once clerical, backward-looking, and ahistorical. What Maritain did in a number of books devoted to modern culture and politics was to make it seem genuinely serviceable as a tool for coping with the problems of the contemporary world, while Gilson, in the long run possibly even more significantly, worked as a historian of philosophy, historicizing both Thomism and the whole range and variety of thought from Augustine to Descartes. In such books as *The Spirit of Medieval Philosophy*, the Gifford Lectures of 1932, and *The Unity of Philosophical Experience* (1937), the William James lectures given at Harvard, he succeeded in making Thomism reappear, even in the eyes of non-Catholics, as a system of thought that could be taken with full seriousness in the 20th century. The development of a school of Anglican Thomist theologians, including Austin Farrer and Eric Mascall, shows how impressive this could appear.

But it was not only on the strictly philosophical front that Catholicism was once more influencing Anglicanism. The liturgical movement that had developed in France and Belgium from the early years of the century, to recover lay participation as against the highly clericalized liturgy that had characterized the Catholic Church for generations, had important reverberations across the English Channel in works like A. G. Hebert's edited volume, *The Parish Communion* (1937). Equally important in both churches was a wider revival of ecclesiology, demonstrated in Catholicism by the 'rediscovery' of the idea of the church as

Christ's 'mystical body' and in Anglicanism by Michael Ramsey's little masterpiece, *The Gospel and the Catholic Church* (1936), which brought together a whole range of developments: the 'biblical theology' deriving from the Barthian counter-attack against the liberal belittlement of biblical themes with new Catholic insights into liturgy and the church as Christ's Body.

Upon the Protestant side, the 1930s were increasingly dominated by the challenge of Nazism. Within Germany this produced division between the majority whose nationalism undercut any serious resistance and a minority, originally inspired by Barth and marshalled increasingly by Dietrich Bonhoeffer, who produced the Barmen Declaration (1934), insisting on the reality and freedom of the church *vis à vis* the state, which led to the formation of the 'Confessing Church'. Internationally it was the threat of Nazism, Fascism, and Communism which did much to stimulate the advance of the ecumenical movement and the decision to merge the two networks entitled Faith and Order and Life and Work into a proposed World Council of Churches. The basic decisions here were taken in 1937 at the two movements' conferences in Oxford and Edinburgh. The Oxford Conference of Life and Work in July on 'Church, Community, and the State' in particular brought together a highly impressive range of Christian thinkers and church leaders of many countries, concerned to map out the social significance of Christianity in the modern world. It is impossible to imagine so serious a theological conference or such a subject, with committees on Church and State, Economics, War, and similar themes, at any much earlier date. The Oxford Conference marks a decisive turn in the history of modern Christian thinking, completely outdating the individualist piety and uncritical nationalism of a Harnack. The only comparably weighty precedent can be found in papal encyclicals from Leo XIII's *Rerum Novarum* on. Perhaps the key theological figure here was Reinhold Niebuhr, but the presence of Barthians or near-Barthians like Hendrik Kraemer and Emil Brunner, as well as of a range of lay intellectuals, from A. D. Lindsay, at the time Oxford University's Vice-Chancellor, to Sir Walter Moberly,

Foster Dulles, T. S. Eliot, and distinguished people from almost every part of the globe, including many Eastern Orthodox, pointed towards the emergence of something fairly describable as a new Christian intellectual community, emphatic in its commitment to the creeds, but powerful especially in its sense of mission to the world of economics and politics. In this sense of mission one should again note a new preoccupation with the church as such. 'The first duty of the Church, and its greatest service to the world, is that it be in very deed the Church', declared the conference message, striking a Barthian note. Yet one may note also a degree of consensus about natural law and natural theology. Barth indeed was not at Oxford, and his one great division with Brunner, who was there, lay in Brunner's acceptance of the validity of natural theology. Barth had, in his tempestuous way, already written his *Nein! Antwort an Emil Brunner* on this point. It would continue to divide Christian thinkers sharply, but the strong acceptance of the idea of natural law by many, as, for instance, William Temple, at that time archbishop of York and more than anyone else the guiding spirit at Oxford, would again serve to bring the central direction of non-Catholic theology back towards a more Catholic viewpoint. While there were no Catholics at Oxford, the influence of Maritain and Christopher Dawson was considerable.

There were also no German delegates at Oxford. Those who had hoped to come were prevented from doing so and Martin Niemöller was arrested just before the conference began. But the theologian who more than anyone else would in retrospect come to represent the decisive move in 20th-century theology signified by the Oxford conference was a German, Dietrich Bonhoeffer. He too had been a pupil of Harnack; he had then come under the influence of both Barth and Niebuhr. More than any of these, he struggled as a Lutheran to a position of such full involvement in the political that he became part of the conspiracy to overthrow Hitler and was hanged just before the fall of the Nazi regime. While the turning towards a theology of politics took very different forms with Barth, Niebuhr, Temple, and Bonhoeffer, the construction of a new vision of church–state relations of a non-nationalist kind was important for all of them, and it would remain important for the rest of the century, despite something of a lull in concern in the 1950s.

The Second World War delayed the launching of the World Council of Churches until 1948 but ensured that when it came it received very wide support from almost all the non-Roman communions. If neither Barth nor the leading Anglican Michael Ramsey attended the 1937 conferences, both took a very active part at Amsterdam in 1948. While the World Council claimed to impose no ecclesiology upon the churches, it inevitably both stimulated its members to think about ecclesiology—why, precisely, as churches, they were divided—and forged a largely new kind of theological community which twelve years later the Catholic Church too would join. While in the Protestant world the 1950s saw the continued dominance of pre-war theologians—Barth, Bultmann, Tillich, the Niebuhrs—in the Catholic world the post-war years witnessed new developments that would prove enormously important. In 1950 the leading inspirer of the French Dominican school of the Saulchoir in Paris, M. D. Chenu, published his *Introduction à l'étude de saint Thomas d'Aquin*, a work reflecting twenty years of teaching in the richness of its ability to interpret Aquinas within his historical milieu, the Paris of seven centuries earlier. Why does this matter so much? Because it challenged the still-dominant ahistorical approach to Thomism, regarded as a system belonging to all ages and therefore understandable outside its historical setting. While Gilson had propagated a historicist approach to scholasticism, he had confined himself to the field of philosophy where, as a layman, he did not seem to threaten current theological method too evidently. It was the transference of this approach to theology, something Chenu had already begun with his little 1937 work, *Une école de théologie: Le Saulchoir*, which made the alarm bells ring. It was not that Chenu doubted the supreme intellectual genius of Aquinas. On the contrary, he wanted it understood, but, when placed within its historical milieu, it must require rethinking in every other milieu. Once this line was followed, the underlying post-Tridentine assumption of Catholic theology, that nothing much that mattered had happened either before or after Thomas, was shattered. Chenu's younger colleague Yves Congar was applying this approach in a variety of ways. His *Chrétiens désunis* (1937) opened up the issue of Catholic ecumenism in a truly foundational way while his *Vraie et fausse réforme dans l'Église* (1950) appealed for a fundamental reform of the church through a 'return to the sources'. Both the Dominican theologians of the Saulchoir and another remarkable group of Jesuit theologians centred on their house in Lyons and inspired by Henri de Lubac, whose interests were more patristic, were soon creating a far more diversified theology than the Catholic Church had known for centuries. De Lubac's works on the Eucharist and the Mystical Body (1944) and, still more, *Surnaturel* (1946), his studies of allegory, making much use of Origen, of atheistic humanism, and Buddhism, all published in these years, appeared to challenge aspect after aspect of the current Catholic theological framework.

There had, inevitably, to be a reaction. The Dominican Toulouse province had long been more rigidly Thomist than that of Paris. In 1946 the *Revue Thomiste*, for which it was responsible, published a critique of the work of the Lyons Jesuits—de Lubac, Daniélou, Bouillard, von Balthasar—to which they quickly responded. Further articles followed, all to be included by M.-J. Nicolas and M.-M. Labourdette, the editors of the *Revue Thomiste*, the following year in a work entitled *Dialogue théologique*. Rather than dialogue it looked like denunciation. For the Toulouse school the 'rigorously scientific character of theology' was at stake. The fondness of the Jesuits for patristic sources demonstrated a 'clear depreciation of scholastic theology', a move towards 'relativism', a lack of true 'fidelity to St Thomas'. The Saulchoir too, by implication, was under attack. In 1950 Pope Pius XII condemned all these tendencies, which had come to be known as the 'nouvelle théologie', though without mentioning names, in the encyclical *Humani Generis* which looked somewhat like a repeat of *Pascendi*. Chenu and Congar in Paris, de Lubac and others in Lyons, were soon removed from their teaching posts. The last great battle against every form of 'modernism' was being waged, but this time it was destined to be lost. There was too much to suppress, and theologians like Congar and de Lubac were too clearly outstanding scholars and devout priests to be discredited. Even Rome itself was divided. Overt anti-modernists like Pietro Parente, Assessor of the Holy Office and then cardinal archbishop of Perugia, had turned their attacks on fellow Romans, such as the Jesuit, Paul Galtier, of the Gregorianum, for his neo-Nestorian views on the human consciousness of Christ. A vast evolution of theological understanding had in fact been set in motion within Catholicism and nothing could suppress it for long. If, apart from the *Milieu divin*, none of the works of Teilhard de Chardin were allowed to be published in his lifetime, once he died in 1955 they quickly saw the light and exercised a vast influence. He too was a close friend of de Lubac. It is often implied that a great theological revival was unloosed in the Catholic Church by Vatican II. In reality, the best of the revival probably came before the Council was even announced. That was certainly true of France, the real power-house behind all that happened, when combined with the work of German theologians such as Karl Rahner. Important as the role of Pope John XXIII was in closing an era of repression and inaugurating one of openness, almost unprecedented in Roman history, in terms of thought itself his influence should not be exaggerated. Indeed he appeared not too unhappy with the thoroughly reactionary preliminary draft texts produced in Rome for the Council. When in 1962, in the opening session, they were almost all rejected, it was because the impact of the *nouvelle théologie* and related influences (including, indeed, the earlier, more liberal encyclicals of Pius XII, notably *Divino Afflante Spiritu*, 1943, on the interpretation of scripture, and *Mediator Dei*, 1947, on the liturgy) had had an effect far beyond what theologians in Rome imagined.

The impact of Vatican II, nevertheless, in spreading the new ideas and breaking down practices of repression still current in many parts of the church was enormous. It is to be remembered that in many ways the century separating Vatican I from Vatican II had been for Catholicism an enormously productive one. The missionary movement had multiplied Catholics and dioceses in Africa and Asia; the Latin American church had grown still more; in North America Catholicism was now by far the largest single religious body. Everywhere colleges and seminaries had multiplied while the sense of defensive fear, of having the 'true faith' but none the less being an anachronism in the modern, liberal, and Protestant world, still strong at the beginning of the century, had faded away. The church as a whole was ready for intellectual spring-cleaning.

But the impact of Vatican II has also to be seen within the wider culture of the 1960s. Everywhere the 1950s had been a remarkably conservative age: conservatively communist in one part of the globe, conservatively democratic elsewhere. The values of the church too were inherently restorationist, frozen, perhaps, by the tensions of the Cold War. There seemed little new to say, little reflection even on what had happened during the war, including both the Holocaust and Hiroshima. Quite suddenly, as the 1950s turned into the 1960s, this changed and a cultural revolution for a time swept all before it—an optimistic revolution in institutional, intellectual, and sexual attitudes, symbolized as well as anything by President Kennedy's 'Camelot' and the music of the Beatles. 1960 was the 'year of Africa'. The old empires were being hastily wound up and a multitude of new countries were taking their seats at the United Nations. Intellectually, the left seemed to have won—not the tired left of Soviet Marxism, but an exciting new left, fed on the writings of the Young Marx, and a range of Marxist-inclined gurus, from Sartre and Marcuse to Habermas, Ernst Bloch, and Frantz Fanon. Joined to an upsurge of Christian existentialism feeding on a new popularity of the works of Kierkegaard, all this was to have a very considerable impact on Christian thought, but the most striking phenomenon of the new religious radicalism, John Robinson's *Honest to God* (1963), owed less to such influences, being an amalgam of ideas derived from Bultmann, Tillich, and Bonhoeffer. What might least be expected was the third. Bonhoeffer had not been a major theological name in his lifetime. As his biographer, Eberhard Bethge, wrote in 1970, 'In 1945 only a handful of friends and enemies knew who this young man had been. In Christian Germany other names were in the limelight. When his name began to emerge from the anonymity of his death, theological faculties and churches felt uncertain and did little. To the present day there are still inhibitions in Germany about fully integrating him and what he stood for' (Preface to English edition of *Dietrich Bonhoeffer*). What excited the 1960s about Bonhoeffer was not just his role as a conspirator against Hitler, but the *Letters and Papers from Prison* which suddenly became, often indeed through misinterpretation, a sort of contemporary gospel of 'religionless Christianity'. *Honest to God* sold more than a million copies and, while it infuriated many firm believers, deeply influenced numerous waverers. This mix of what Barth is unkindly said to have described as the 'froth', mixed together from the 'good beers' of Tillich, Bonhoeffer, and Bultmann (and especially the first), was certainly the standard of a revival of 'liberal' theology over against the previous Barth-dominated years.

The world of 1963 saw not only *Honest to God* but also the height of excitement over the Vatican Council after the almost revolutionary impression of its first session in autumn 1962. In April came Pope John's encyclical *Pacem in Terris*, addressing the issues of peace among the nations in a nuclear age with remarkable freshness. Two months later he died, but, under his successor Paul VI, his council continued. Little of the teaching of Vatican II constituted in itself a major contribution to Christian thought. It could fairly be said that on many points the Catholic Church was only catching up on what Protestantism had recognized either four centuries or one century earlier, although the Council's most carefully shaped document, *Lumen Gentium*, expressed a richness of ecclesiology not easily found elsewhere. With its shift away from preoccupation with the hierarchical, it represented an acceptable Catholic response to the Protestant rediscovery of ecclesiology since the 1930s. The Council's larger impact was immense in a number of ways. Its longest constitution, *Gaudium et Spes*, on 'the church in the modern world', covered a vast range of matters, political, social, cultural, and economic. While much that was said may appear bland or simplistic, what remains significant was that a council should treat of such matters at all, let alone at such length. Comparably significant was the much argued-over and finally very cautiously worded Declaration, *Nostra Aetate*, on non-Christian religions. What is important in both cases is the opening these documents provided for the future. Still more central to the Council's work was the opening of doors between Catholics and other Christians. This was achieved, first, by the invitation of a considerable number of observers from other churches to attend all the Council's sessions. Their presence greatly influenced what was said. It led on through the work of the new *Secretariat of Unity* to the beginning of numerous official 'dialogues' between Rome and other churches, including the WCC. The result was that whereas up to 1960 there had been extremely limited theological contact anywhere between Catholics and other Christians, now it grew not only officially but unofficially to such an extent that the whole public shape of the Christian thought-world was irretrievably altered within a few years, Catholics and Protestants coming to study and teach in many of the same institutions.

While the debates and even some of the decisions of the Vatican Council seemed radical indeed in the eyes of many Catholics, the 1960s saw the development of far more radical radicalisms elsewhere. The 'Death of God' school flourished particularly in America, beginning with G. Vahanian's *The Death of God* (1961) and continuing with such works as T. J. Altizer's *The Gospel of Christian Atheism* (1966). It grew out of a mixture of Hegel, Nietzsche, Bonhoeffer's *Letters and Papers*, and a belief that analytical philosophy had made discourse about God meaningless. While most theologians were not persuaded by the full message, a general break-up of doctrinal coherence seemed to be going on almost everywhere, even in Catholicism where it was widely felt that Aquinas had had his day and must now be replaced by whatever was available in the current market—Barth or Bultmann,

Rahner or Altizer. The symposium edited by John Hick, *The Myth of God Incarnate* (1978), with its rather overconfident conviction that the doctrine of the Incarnation could be debunked, represents a late expression of this form of radical liberalism by people occupying the most senior academic positions.

But the radicalism of the 1960s took other, some more enduring, forms. The fourth assembly of the WCC, Uppsala 1968, made a move from church-centred to world-centred concerns of a fairly radical sort, both mirroring and going well beyond *Gaudium et Spes*. Not unrelated to the Uppsala agenda were developments in Latin America. One of the changes of shape in Christian geography in the post-Second World War period most productive in the field of thought was the advance of Latin America as a giver, and not only receiver, of ideas. The Conference of Latin American Bishops held at Medellín in 1968, a major influence on the reshaping of the South American church, was intended as a follow-up to the Vatican Council for the continent containing the largest numbers of Catholics. It led to the publication in 1971 in Lima of Gustavo Gutiérrez's *A Theology of Liberation*, which quickly became a classic text, while being the precursor for a great many other works in the same area by such Latin American theologians as Segundo, Sobrino, Míguez Bonino, and Boff. Here was a whole new school of liberation theology coming to grips with the central issues of politics, justice, and empowerment in a particular social context and considerably influenced by Marxist ideology. Undoubtedly they also owed a good deal to the more theoretical development of 'political theology' by Moltmann, J. B. Metz, and others. But liberation theology was more context-shaped. If, with some of its proponents, it represented a large incorporation of Marxist concepts into Christian thought (at times uncritically, at others quite transforming them in the process), this was essentially as a tool for the construction of a public theology relevant to local circumstances and capable of stimulating social change, even revolution. It was thus both a sociopolitical theology and a local theology, the first considerable example of a coherent theological school outside Europe and North America in modern times.

Whether parallel to, or derived from, liberation theology there developed a range of others: black, feminist, African, Dalit, Minjung. Some of these, fairly temporarily, made use of Marxism; for others that would have been pointless or quite unacceptable. They did, of course, overlap. It had suddenly been rediscovered that not only Latin Americans, but also women and Blacks could be good theologians. What all this had in common was commitment to the theological enterprise from a position quite different from that which had dominated theology hitherto: white, western, male, probably clerical, academic, upper middle-class. What they were all saying is that the way one thinks about God, Christ, the bible, the church, and morality depends enormously on where one is and who one is. Both 19th-century 'scientific' Protestant theology and 'perennial' Catholic scholasticism had forgotten that. Truth is just truth, theology just theology. The switch to acceptance of not only the fact but also the appropriateness of pluralism in theology (a switch from seeing theology as modelled on mathematics to seeing it as akin to poetry) has been one of the more enduring acquisitions of the 1960s–1970s.

Another has been the incorporation of Christian theology within reflection on 'religion'. In institutional terms departments of theology have been transformed into or joined with departments of religious studies whose subject is world religions. Until the 1960s the theologian who took any other religion as a significant part of his field of study, as de Lubac took Buddhism, was extremely unusual. Christian theology was carried on against a background of the bible and western history, but with minimal consideration of other religious experience except, as in the case of Barthians such as Kraemer, to condemn it. When this changed, the immediate tendency, represented particularly by Wilfred Cantwell Smith and John Hick, was to declare, in the latter's phraseology, that a 'Copernican revolution' had been achieved making impossible continued belief in the 'uniqueness' of Christ or Christianity. Others, no less sensitive to the implications of the human and religious experience of the large non-Christian majority of the world's population, did not believe that Hick's hasty willingness to throw over the central claims of Christianity was necessary or helpful for understanding the religious predicament as a whole.

Religion and religions, liberalism and the 'Death of God', liberation theology and Marxist historical analysis, feminist theology, Catholic abandonment of Thomism as a privileged system, and much else appeared to leave theology a wreck by the later 1970s, a confused mix of tendencies without any clear centre. Yet the theological history of the last quarter of the 20th century was, surprisingly, very different from that. Central to the 1980s and the 1990s was a considerable recovery of orthodoxy, of a Trinitarian and incarnationalist kind, challenged more by the spread of fundamentalism than by the extreme liberalism of previous decades that somehow failed to stick. It was replaced by what might be called a Nicaean reshaping of Catholic, Orthodox, and Protestant traditions, in which the principal resources are undoubtedly Aquinas, Barth, and the Greek fathers. German Protestant theology has retained its ascendancy, notably through the work of Moltmann, Pannenberg, and Jüngel. While the authority of Bultmann and Tillich has steadily waned, that of Barth has remained remarkably constant, even if it is the later Barth of the *Church Dogmatics*, more willing to be positive about humanity, to which appeal is mostly made. His rejection of 'natural theology' continued to be itself rejected, as notably by Pannenberg, who came to represent the most central position within the Protestant tradition. What is no less striking is the influence of Aquinas. Far from diminishing after Vatican II as anticipated, it has spread very noticeably across the Protestant world. He is now seen not as the formal pillar of Roman Catholic orthodoxy, but rather as the greatest of systematic theologians, yet someone whose teaching has still to be seen as contextually shaped by his own age, one very different from ours. The importance of the Greek fathers is almost as pervasive. It is something shared by the school of Lyons, led by de Lubac and Daniélou, the training ground of von Balthasar, by Barthians like Torrance, and by Greek Orthodox theologians like Kallistos Ware and John Zizioulas. The massive interest in Origen, as in Irenaeus, is evidence of how important the very early patristic witness especially has come to be seen. While Orthodox theology has not played a central role in 20th-century theological thought, it has had an increasingly pervasive influence, from the inter-war writing of such Russian *émigrés* as Berdyaev and Bulgakov in Paris to the ever-wider presence of Greek and Russian Orthodox churches throughout the world, especially in North America.

Yet this reconciliation of the theological centre has by no means involved totally discarding the legacy of the 1960s and 1970s. On the contrary. The continued context of world religions and a socio-ethical agenda set in its main lines by political and liberation theology are not in question. Still more important, explicit diversities of viewpoint resulting in a necessary pluralism of theology have been built into the new scheme of things, including a considerable range of viewpoints across the liberal–orthodox spectrum. The perennial theological tension between rationality and fideism has certainly not disappeared, though it can take on a new look in a world where the values of enlightenment and modernity are under wide attack. The diversities within contemporary theology may be justified by some in postmodernist terms but by others as in reality characteristic of Christian theology throughout its history: the inevitable consequence of a religion of incarnation and of the otherness of people whose response to God's word must be as diverse as the range of human thought and culture. A return to the narrow agenda and western self-satisfaction of the 1950s would be unthinkable, just as any abandonment of the implications of Vatican II would be unthinkable on the Catholic side, despite curial attempts under John Paul II to re-establish something like the theological control of the pre-conciliar era. In general, despite notable weaknesses such as the collapse of the French intellectual leadership which mattered so much to Catholicism in the past, Christian theology may well be in a healthier, more internally coherent, and less schismatic state than has been the case for many centuries.

Bowden, J., and Richmond, J. (eds.), *A Reader in Contemporary Theology* (1967).

The Catechism of the Catholic Church, ET (1994).

Chopp, R., *The Praxis of Suffering: An Interpretation of Liberation and Political Theologies* (1986).

Clements, K., *Lovers of Discord: Twentieth-Century Theological Controversies in England* (1988).

Fabella, V., and Torres, S. (eds.), *Irruption of the Third World: Challenge to Theology* (1983).

Ford, D. F. (ed.), *The Modern Theologians* (2nd edn., 1997).

Gill, R. (ed.), *Readings in Modern Theology* (1995).

Hastings, A., *A History of English Christianity 1920–1999* (2000).

——— (ed.), *Modern Catholicism* (1991).

Hastings, C., and Nicholl, D. (eds.), 'A Correspondence: Adolf Harnack and Erik Peterson', *Selection I* (1953), 169–85.

Heron, A., *A Century of Protestant Theology* (1980).

Hodgson, H., and King, R. (eds.), *Christian Theology: An Introduction to its Traditions and Tasks* (1982).

Loades, A., *Searching for Lost Coins: Explorations in Christianity and Feminism* (1987).

Mackey, J., *Modern Theology: A Sense of Direction* (1987).

Macquarrie, J., *Twentieth-Century Religious Thought* (4th edn.; 1988).

Moltmann, J., *Theology Today* (1988).

Pauck, W., *Harnack and Troeltsch* (1968).

Rumscheidt, H. M., *Revelation and Theology: An Analysis of the Barth-Harnack Correspondence of 1923* (1972).

Schoof, T., *A Survey of Catholic Theology 1800–1970* (1970).

Streeter, B. H. (ed.), *Foundations* (1912).

Tracy, D., *Blessed Rage for Order: The New Pluralism in Theology* (1975).

Tyrrell, G., *Medievalism: A Reply to Cardinal Mercier*, new edn. with foreword by Gabriel Daly (1994).

von Harnack, A., *What is Christianity?* (1901).

Wilmore, G. S., and Cone, J. (eds.), *Black Theology: A Documentary History 1966–1979* (1979).